By the same author
Evington Parish Church
Discovering Leicester

To my family

Copyright
© JOHN W. BANNER 1994
I.S.B.N. 0 90167 520 2

Published by Leicester City Council
Living History Unit.

OUT AND ABOUT IN LEICESTER

CONTENTS

Introduction 5

Chapter 1
    St. Nicholas Circle, St. Nicholas Place, Applegate, Guildhall Lane, St. Martins West, St. Martins, St. Martins East, Loseby Lane, Carts Lane, High Street, Highcross Street. 7

Chapter 2
    St. Nicholas Circle, Castle Gardens, The Newarke, Castle View, Castle Precincts, The Newarke, Southgates, Friar Lane, Berridge Street, Horsefair Street, Town Hall Square, Horsefair Street 31

Chapter 3
    Granby Street, Gallowtree Gate, Clock Tower, Humberstone Gate, Humberstone Road, Humberstone Gate, Church Gate, St. Margaret's Church, Church Gate, East Gates, Cheapside, Market Place, Hotel Street. 49

Chapter 4
    Bowling Green Street, Belvoir Street, Welford Place, King Street, New Walk, University Road, Regent Road, King Street, Welford Place, Pocklington's Walk. 69

Chapter 5
    Granby Street, London Road, Victoria Park, University, University Road, Welford Road, Almond Road, Aylestone Road, Infirmary Road, Oxford Street, Newarke Street. 85

  Bibliography 107

  Index 109

Leicester Guildhall Courtyard. *(Leicester City Council)*

OUT AND ABOUT IN LEICESTER

INTRODUCTION

Many people lead such busy lives that they have no time to look higher than a shop's windows, which is a pity for even to the casual observer there is so much of interest to find out about Leicester. For example consider the following questions:

What was that stone building in Granby Street with the wonderful dome built for?
Is it true that a chapel had to be pulled down to build the station?
Where is Top Hat Terrace and how did it get that name?
Why did Richard III have to stay in a common inn when he came to Leicester in 1485?

The questions that could be asked are endless and many of the answers are to be found in the pages of this book.

I was among the first group of City Guides to receive training, qualify, and be awarded the coveted guides' Blue Badge. For ten years I took parties of interested people on guided walks around various parts of the city. When the onset of arthritis took its toll I could no longer do this work though I was still able to give talks on Leicester's history. It occurred to me that there must be many people who are interested in the past who are unable to join a party on a guided walk either through illness, infirmity, or advancing years. There may be others too who are interested but do not wish to make the effort!

It is for all these individuals and others who might have lived in Leicester but have now moved away, that I have written this book. I want you to imagine you are being taken on a guided walk following a preordained route and I have tried to give as much information as I could about all the interesting places we encounter as we go along. There are five armchair tours: I suggest that you take them one at a time and perhaps find out more information for yourself afterwards. After all, even a City Guide cannot know everything!

I have listed many of my sources in the bibliography, but much of my information has been gathered over so many years that it is impossible to give credit where it is due, but I am grateful to everyone who has helped.

Happy armchair touring!

John W. Banner
Markfield
January 1994

OUT AND ABOUT IN LEICESTER

CHAPTER ONE

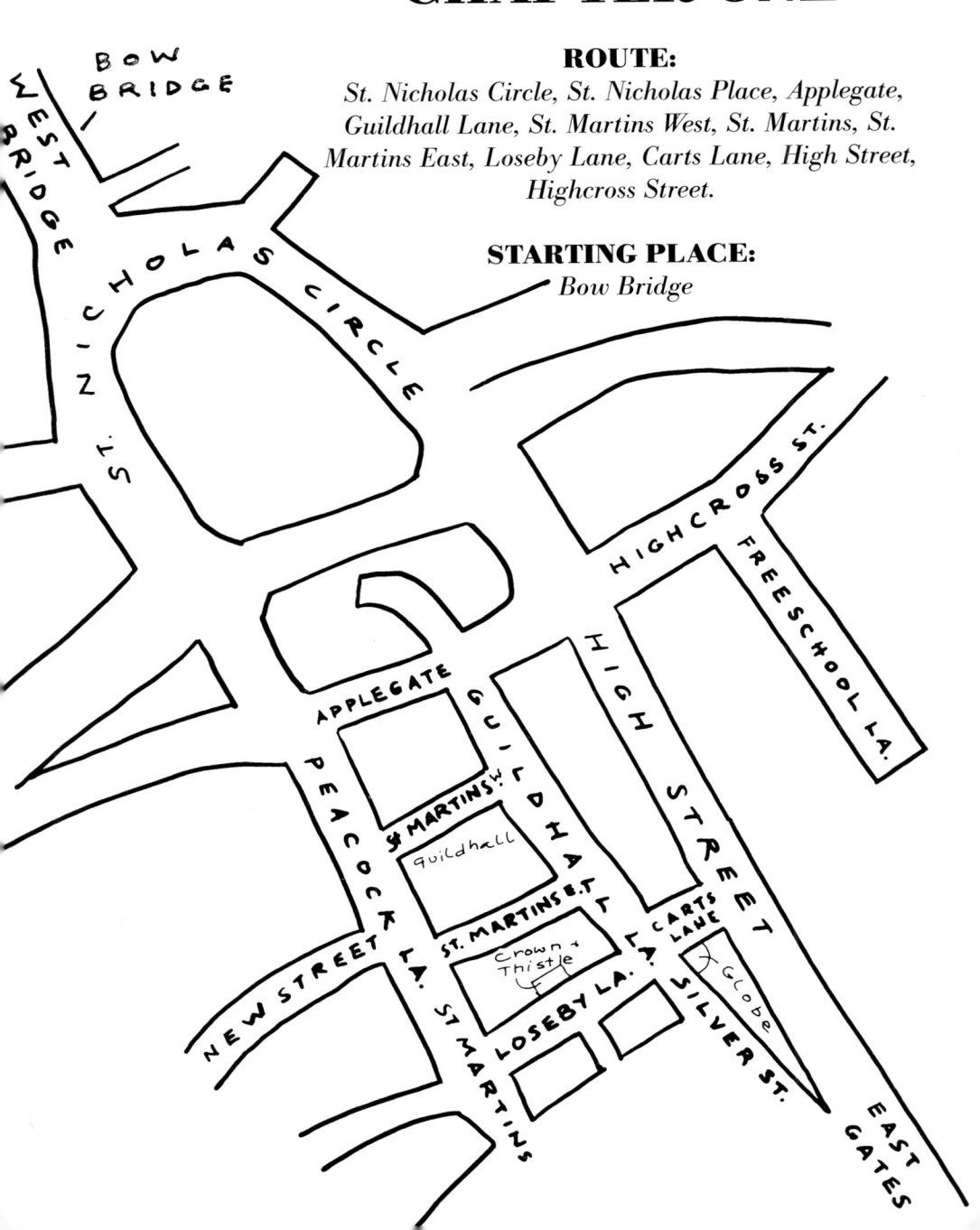

ROUTE:
St. Nicholas Circle, St. Nicholas Place, Applegate, Guildhall Lane, St. Martins West, St. Martins, St. Martins East, Loseby Lane, Carts Lane, High Street, Highcross Street.

STARTING PLACE:
Bow Bridge

Detail of mermaid panel, West Bridge. *(Leicester City Council)*

Just in front of us as we stand on **BOW BRIDGE** is the site of Leicester's Augustinian Friary. The Austin Friars arrived in Leicester in the mid 13th century and we still remember them from the name given to St. Augustine's Road. The River Soar has several branches in this area and the Friary buildings stood on an island formed by the river which is crossed firstly by Bow Bridge and then by West Bridge as we approach the City. The friars lived by begging and devoted their lives to good works among the people and to preaching, so their churches were always fairly large. Unfortunately, because it was so near to the town, stone from the Friary church and domestic premises was robbed for building materials after its dissolution in 1538 and little evidence of its existence was to be found above ground: substantial excavations in 1973-78 however gave us a good picture of the extent of the buildings. In 1830 the terminus station of the Leicester and Swannington Railway Company was built on the site of the Friary. This railway, design by Robert Stephenson was the first to be constructed in the Midlands.

A plaque at the side of the bridge parapet tells us that the Mayor, Alderman Viccars, opened it in 1862 so it is by no means the first bridge on this site, in fact is has been rebuilt several times. It takes its name from an earlier bridge which was bow-shaped. It is said that when Richard III, en route to Bosworth Field, crossed over the bridge on 21 August 1485 at the head of his soldiers he struck his foot on the corner stone: an old woman who stood nearby foretold that when he next crossed the river here his head would be banged on the same corner stone. The story goes that after he had been killed at Bosworth Field his naked body was thrown over the back of a

Old Bow Bridge c. 1860. *(From Read R., Modern Leicester 1881)*

horse and his head did indeed strike the corner stone as he was brought back into Leicester. There is an interesting sequel to this story: at the time of the Reformation Richard's tomb was broken up and his bones were flung over Bow Bridge into the river. Around 1830 Henry Goddard, founder of the well known family consisting of five generations of Leicester architects, found two skulls under a pier while overseeing the reconstruction of Bow Bridge. One skull had a massive cleft through the cranium and the other was unmutilated. Over twenty years ago the skulls were carbon-dated and were confirmed to be of male origin and roughly 500 years old. The first one now rests on a velvet mount in a country house and the Goddard family still have the unmutilated skull, kept in the safety of a bank vault. Did one of them belong to Richard III? We shall never know.

Cast in the iron of the bridge parapet are panels bearing the arms of the king, supported by two white boars (the white boar was his badge), and his motto *Loyaute Me Lie* - Fidelity Binds Me. Other panels bear the white rose of York. Note the panel let into the wall near the bridge bearing the message *Near this spot lie the remains of Richard III, last of the Plantagenets, 1485.* This panel was built into the wall of a factory by the riverside in 1856 and was removed to its present position when the factory was pulled down.

A few yards further on, on the left, is an attractive brick-built feature with a large circular opening in the centre decorated by sculptures of **MERMAIDS** in the two upper sections. The sculptures were moulded by hand in terracotta by William Neatby in 1900 at the Lambeth Pottery of Doulton & Co. They originally formed a decorative feature of the entrance to the old Wholesale Fish, Fruit and Vegetable Market in Rutland Street and were preserved when the market was demolished in 1972.

Across the road, overlooking the Soar, is Whitmore's worsted spinning mill, later the Pex factory, built in 1844; with its classical proportions and row of dormer windows it is perhaps the finest of the surviving buildings designed by William Flint, the prominent Leicester architect.

Onwards now to **WEST BRIDGE** at one of the most important entrances to both the Roman and medieval towns. In Roman times this was the only place where the bed of the river was firm enough for it to be forded. The first bridge on this site was built by Robert de Beaumont, who was the first Earl of Leicester from 1107 to 1118, and it has been re-built a number of times since then. A chapel dedicated to St. Mary de Brigge or Our Lady of the Bridge was built on the bridge in 1365. Two Austin friars from the nearby Friary used to stand by the entrance begging alms from passers by until the Reformation brought the dissolution of monastic establishments: in 1598 the chapel was converted into a house and then it became a barber's shop until 1841 when it was demolished along with the bridge. When the bridge was re-built the foundations of the early Norman bridge were found.

The present bridge, known as the John Butler bridge, was built in 1891 at a cost of £4,000: note the heads of Chaucer's Canterbury pilgrims, superbly carved in stone, on the pillars. A second bridge was built alongside in 1982 to create a dual carriageway. It was here that Daniel Lambert, Leicester's famous fat man, used to take a weekly swim in the river; it was said that his great bulk gave him added buoyancy: sometimes he would swim with two men on his back and take great delight in capsizing them. It was at this place too that scolds were ducked.

Leicester's industry was enabled to develop when the Leicester Navigation, which passes beneath West Bridge, was completed in 1794. The cost of transporting coal, which used to be carried by pack horses, was greatly reduced making its use economic for domestic purposes and, later in the 19th Century, for generating steam for factories: coal was now cheap enough to be used for making gas and for smelting pig iron and the canal opened up an easy way for an export trade via the Trent and Humber. The first part of the Leicester Navigation terminated at West Bridge and letters cut into the kerb stones a few hundred yards north of the bridge mark the spot. In medieval times wood for fuel used to be brought from Leicester Forest by way of West Bridge. A penny was the toll charged for a horse's load and a farthing for a man's load. The **WEST GATE** used to stand on the town side of West Bridge and its location is now marked by a Blue Plaque. The street running in the direction of the town was called Applegate Street. This was perhaps the most important of Leicester's gates where visitors were usually welcomed. A keen lookout would be posted on one of the gate's towers to watch for their approach and to look out for strangers who would be closely examined and turned back if they were suffering from some disease, particularly plague, or were known criminals. At the sign of any trouble the watchman would call for help from the Castle which was only a few hundred yards away. The Norman Earls and their retinue spoke Norman French and the French word for a call is appel. Gata is a Danish word meaning 'a road' - hence Applegate means 'the road of the call'. To add 'street' to the name was something of a misnomer, equivalent to saying 'Appel Road Street'.

In common with the town's other three gates the west gate was of massive construction and had a drawbridge and a portcullis for additional security. We have no illustrations of the gates but by studying the Chamberlains' accounts for materials for their repair it is possible to get some idea of how they were built. For example there are items for tiles so the gates must have had pitched roofs: from entries for door hinges it is clear that each gate had two huge doors with a wicket gate in each. The cost of painting the royal arms is recorded, making it clear that these were borne on each gate. Interestingly there are entries for re-painting them at the times of the Commonwealth and the Restoration. The gates were like fortresses with battlements, guardrooms, walkways and dungeons above the gates themselves. As years went by the town walls and gates were unnecessary for defence though the gates made it easy to collect tolls from traders coming into the town. From time to time an unpopular tax known as murage was levied for the repair of both walls and gates: the walls were the first to disappear and the rooms above the gates were let as living accommodation until they too were pulled down in 1774. They were sold by auction for building materials because they were too low and too narrow for farm vehicles and coaches to pass through.

On our right is an entrance to the Castle Gardens now part of the city's Castle Park. Facing us is the Holiday Inn: before this was built and Applegate Street disappeared as St. Nicholas Circle was created, this area was known as Everard Place and the bronze statue of the Duke of Rutland now in the Market Place stood on a small island facing the river.

We turn left now and climb the steps to the terrace which leads to the Vaughan College entrance - we can get a better view of the **JEWRY WALL** from here. This relic from the ancient town is the largest upstanding piece of Roman masonry in the country: it may have survived because it was once incorporated into a Saxon church: but let us go back a little earlier. The Romans landed on the coast of Kent in 43 A.D. and overcame the Celtic tribes as they advanced northwards to the Thames where, by arrangement, they awaited the arrival of the Emperor Claudius.

They crossed the river and made their way to Camulodunum (roughly where Colchester is today) and conquered the Catuvelauni. They proceeded northwards along a rough track, which was later to become the Via Devana, and entered the site of present day Leicester along the line of New Walk. On a mound of sand and gravel where the Holiday Inn now stands they found a settlement of Celtic people called the 'Corieltauvi'. The Romans called the settlement 'Ratae Corieltauvorum'. 'Ratae' means 'ramparts' - earthern banks thrown up for defence, and 'Corieltauvorum' means 'of the Corieltauvi'. They built a fort on the town side of the river to protect the intersection of the Fosse Way, the Via Devana and the ford: as tribes further north were conquered the Roman army was withdrawn, the fort was dismantled and the land was handed over for civilian use towards the end of the first century. By this time the Corieltauvi had become reconciled to Roman administration and Ratae became a 'civitas' capital - a town of non-Roman citizens who adopted the customs of the invaders and worshiped Roman gods.

Erection of public buildings began between 120 and 125 A.D. They were planned by Roman architects and streets were laid out in grid fashion by Roman surveyors. A site was reserved for the Forum to be built some years later where the Southgates Underpass is today. Its open area was used as a market place and a place of public assembly: it was surrounded by colonnades and shops on three sides. The buildings had massive foundations of granite from Groby, Mountsorrel and Enderby: the columns and plinths were carved from millstone grit from Melbourne, Derbyshire, probably transported by boat along the river. On its northern side was a basilica or

Living History Unit
Arts Advisory Section
Leicester City Council
Freepost (LE 985/34)
LEICESTER   LE1 7ZA

The Living History Unit hopes that you have enjoyed this publication. It would be very helpful if you could take a few minutes to complete and return this Freepost Card (no stamp required). Thank you for your help.

Which Living History Unit publication have you bought?..

Where did you buy this publication?..

How would you describe it?   Very interesting ☐   Interesting ☐   Not interesting ☐

Other comments..

Which part of Leicester do you live in?..

How would you describe your ethnic origin?   White ☐   Asian ☐   African Caribbean ☐   Chinese ☐   Other ☐

What is your sex & age?   Male ☐   Female ☐   Under 18 ☐   18-30 ☐   30-60 ☐   60+ ☐

Are you a disabled person?   Yes ☐   No ☐

What other subjects of local history would you like to see published?..

If you would like further information about the Living History Unit, please write your name and address below

....
....

Leicester City Council

civic hall and a Court of Justice stood next to it, roughly where St. Nicholas Church is now. A wall was built round the town which covered an area of about 100 acres. The lines of Roman and medieval walls appear to coincide and it is probable that stone from the former was used for the latter. When excavations were made for the Holiday Inn what was thought to be a Temple of Mithras of the second century A.D. was found: it had a sunken nave and two aisles. Mithras was a Persian god favoured by the officer class of the Roman army.

Many houses had beautiful mosaic floors and some of these can be seen in the museum beneath where we are standing. The one known as the Blackfriars Pavement is said to be one of the finest found in the country. It takes its name from the site of the Blackfriars Friary which stood where the pavement was found when the Great Central railway station was being built - a special chamber had to be constructed for it beneath the station: it was moved to the museum when the railway was closed. Many will remember the mosaic pavement which could be seen in situ in the cellar of a corset shop nearby; this is in the museum along with the so called 'cherry orchard' pavement from the villa excavated in Norfolk Street and the 'Cyparissus' pavement found near All Saints Church. Also on display are good examples of fresco wall paintings and many interesting Roman remains including a milestone.

There followed a period of repair and renewal and when the Romans finally departed their buildings were used as a stone quarry. The walls of some must have remained standing into the medieval period and we see substantial remains in front of us today.

The Jewry Wall is 30 feet high and is built in typical Roman style with a

The Jewry Wall and St Nicholas Church (Leicester City Council)

number of different types of stone including gritstone from Derbyshire: courses of tiles bond the courses. The wall has a core of rubble: the square holes were for the builders' scaffolding. It survives because in the ninth century it was linked structurally with a Saxon church much of which still exists inside St. Nicholas Church.

The name of the wall has an interesting origin - it is thought that 'Jewry' is a corruption of 'Jurats': the Jurats were the 24 senior members of the Borough Corporation who used to meet in the Moot Hall in Blue Boar Lane 'near the Town Churchyard' (presumably St. Nicholas) between the thirteenth and fifteenth centuries and the wall would become known as the 'Jurats' Wall', since corrupted to its present name. In the Middle Ages it was also called the 'Temple of Janus' (the Roman god with two faces).

In the nineteenth century a factory stood on the site and the arches were filled with brickwork. Old drawings from an earlier period show cottages built into the wall. In 1936 the factory was cleared away for the building of swimming baths and the foundations of Roman buildings that we can see in front of us were discovered. Dr. Kathleen Kenyon, a distinguished archaeologist, was placed in charge of the excavations until 1939. She thought the site of the Forum had been found and for some years notices proclaimed it to be 'The Roman Forum'. It was decided to preserve the site and because the war intervened the City had to wait thirty years for its new swimming baths. What had been found were the **ROMAN BATHS** - not swimming baths, but more like Turkish baths. Bathers would pass through one of the central arches to enter a concourse - the long room immediately in front of the Jewry Wall: this was probably a *'frigidarium'* - a cold room. On either side of this concourse are groups of three rooms - changing rooms. One room in the northern block is a latrine with a drain which ran down to the river. The middle three rooms were *'tepidaria'* - warm rooms and two of the rooms nearest to the museum were *'calidaria'* - hot rooms, each of which had hot and cold plunge baths. The centre room was probably a *'laconium'*, a steam room. Bathers would undress, pass through the frigidarium and the tepidaria and go into one of the calidaria. After a time in the hot room they would pass into the steamy laconium and having perspired profusely would apply oil liberally to their bodies and scrape off the sweat and surplus oil with a curved blade of bone or bronze called a strigil. A hot plunge then a cold one would follow. The bathers would then retire to the tepidaria which were like lounges; here they could relax in the warmth before dressing and going out. The whole process was no doubt very leisurely for this was a great place for exchanging news and gossip. Separate times were allotted for men and women. There were three furnaces, one at the end of each of the two calidaria and the other at the end of the laconium. They were built outside to reduce the risk from fire and their remains are now beneath the museum.

Water for the baths and for general use was brought by an aqueduct known as the Raw Dykes, part of which still remains, from Knighton Brook,

1¼ miles from Ratae. It was fed into a reservoir, now under the museum, from which it would be pumped into water towers. After use water was run off from the baths through a drain and into the River Soar. It was also drawn from wells - one was found near the temple on the Holiday Inn site.

The main entrance to the **VAUGHAN COLLEGE** is on our left. The College is the University of Leicester's Department of Adult Education: it takes its name from Canon David J. Vaughan, a vicar of St. Martin's Church, who founded it in 1862 as the Working Men's College with premises in Union Street. The previous Vaughan College building in Great Central Street was swept away when the Southgates Underpass was created.

Having seen **ST. NICHOLAS CHURCH** in the distance beyond the Roman baths, let us take a closer look at it. There is no sign now of the Jewry Wall having been incorporated in the church building but there may have been an earlier Saxon church on this site. The nave of the present church is clearly Saxon - one can see the typical alternating long and short stones of the period on the corner outside. The Leicester diocese was first established in 679 A.D. but had to be abandoned in the 870s when the heathen Danes invaded. It used to be thought that St. Nicholas was Leicester's first Cathedral. Long Saxon windows with arches of Roman titles still remain in the walls of the north side of the nave - they were cut through by the Normans when they built north and south aisles, inserting their usual semi-circular arches. There were similar arches in the south wall but these were removed when the huge brick arch was built in 1829. The clerestory and tower are Norman; the diagonal marks of axes with which the masons worked the stone and their masons' marks can still be seen under the tower. Looking upwards the arcading inside the tower is most impressive. The Normans robbed the decaying Roman buildings to obtain building materials: Roman tiles can be seen incorporated in the outside of the tower. Their chancel and south aisle were replaced in the thirteenth century in the Early English style. The north aisle was found to be unsafe in 1697 and was demolished: it was rebuilt in 1875 in memory of W. Perry-Herrick of Beaumanor Hall.

After the Reformation royal arms were ordered to be placed in all churches and the arms of George II hang in this church. Two bells stand on the floor; they have not been rung for over a century but, as antiquities, they have to be preserved. The church used to have a spire but this had to be taken down in 1805 after being damaged by wind. The sixteenth century timber porch was brought from St. Ursula's Chapel of Wyggeston's Hospital in 1875. In the churchyard are one or two pillars - relics of the Roman Forum, carved in gritstone. There are gravestones too with double dates from the time the calendar was changed from the Justinian to the Gregorian pattern.

On the north side of St. Nicholas Church is a short street with the unusual name of **HOLY BONES**. The original street bearing this name was

Wygston's House *(Leicester City Council)*

destroyed when the Southgates Underpass was made and to preserve the name it was transferred to a part of Jewry Wall Street. Its origin is interesting. The street now called St. Nicholas Place used to be Shambles Lane: in years gone by the butchers shops were here and bones used to accumulate; it was near the church - hence the name 'Holy Bones'.

Let us cross St. Nicholas Circle at the traffic lights and turn right into what used to be a part of Highcross Street but is now 'Applegate' - re-named to preserve that ancient name. Notice on the left a building with encaustic tiles let into the brickwork of the upper walls. It was designed by an architect bearing the memorable name of Francis Drake and was first owned by Swain & Paddy and then by Swain, Almond and Latchmore: they were wholesale grocers, cheese merchants and cigar manufacturers. Look for their initials 'S. A. & L.' on the wrought iron gates.

On the right is **WYGSTON'S HOUSE** the oldest dwelling house in the city - traditionally the home of Roger Wygston, a wool merchant, who was the uncle of William Wyggeston who is commemorated by a statue on the Clock Tower. Roger exported wool to the Flemish weavers through the staple port of Calais, then an English possession. (All wool had to be exported through certain staple ports to ensure that royal taxes were collected).

The half-timbered house was built at the end of the fifteenth century: it used to be L-shaped but the section fronting Applegate was demolished and rebuilt in the Georgian style in 1796. Timber for medieval houses was cut in the forest, shaped while still green and used while still in that state. Consequently as it dried out it would twist, crack and warp: this is one cause of the irregular shape of many old timber buildings. Wygston's house is no exception: it has a row of long narrow vertical window frames which used to be glazed with medieval painted glass. The panes were taken out long ago and the window frames have twisted so much that the glass could not be put back even if this was thought to be wise. Fortunately the glass has been saved; it was sold to the Vicar of Belgrave at the beginning of the nineteenth century and most of the panes are displayed in the Jewry Wall museum. It is beautifully painted with scenes from the life of the Virgin Mary and representations of the various sacraments. Many panels bear the initials 'R.W.', presumably those of Roger Wygston. This is one of the best collections of secular coloured glass in England.

The interior of the house has been expertly restored to its original form and is now the Museum of Costume which is well worth a visit: it has displays of dress down the ages and there is a draper's shop of around the 1920s and other period displays.

Facing Wygston's House on the corner of Applegate and Guildhall Lane we see a building bearing the name 'Wyggeston Hospital Boys' School.' Built in 1876 this was the earliest part of Wyggeston School; it was extended in 1897 as far as the corner of Applegate and Peacock Lane. It had a famous headmaster, Canon James Went, who was head for 42 years until the school was moved to its present site near the University in 1919. He was succeeded by a headmaster named Kingdom and the pupils used to say 'James Went and Kingdom came'! The James Went Building of the De Montfort University is named after him. Alderman Newton Boys' School then occupied the premises and now they form the private Leicester Grammar School.

Now we turn left into Guildhall Lane which was called Town Hall Lane in the nineteenth century and before that Holy Rood Lane until the end of the seventeenth century. 'The Queen's Head', a coaching inn, stood on the corner of St. Martin's East and Town Hall Lane. When the new Town Hall was opened in 1876 the inn lost its trade and the premises were greatly altered to create offices.

The **GUILDHALL** is Leicester's finest medieval building. The Gild of Corpus Christi, which was founded in 1343, built it as their meeting place. The Gild was the richest in the town: its members were the principal businessmen and their wives. It was self-perpetuating - any vacancies were filled by the existing members. Successive outbreaks of bubonic plague in the second half of the fourteenth century caused a setback but by the early fifteenth century it had regained its prosperity and its membership exceeded a hundred. Its chapel was the Lady Chapel of St. Martin's Church (now the Cathedral). The great event of the year was the procession on the Feast of Corpus Christi when the Mayor and other dignitaries, wearing their scarlet robes, were followed by the Gild's four chantry priests bearing the Host aloft beneath a splendidly adorned canopy. A feast concluded the day's ceremonial.

The Gild was closely associated with the government of the Borough its two wardens had powers of arbitration with the Mayor to deal with disputes between members of the Corporation. It was dissolved at the Reformation under the terms of the Chantry Act of 1548.

Most members of the Borough Corporation were also members of the Gild and from 1495 the Corporation used their hall for their meetings, known as 'Common Halls'. When the Gild was dissolved the Corporation bought the hall for £25.15s.4d. - the conveyance, dated 1563, still survives - and it became the Town Hall until the move was made to the present Town Hall in 1876.

The oldest part of the Guildhall - the first three bays to the right of the entrance - was built with cruck timbers between 1350 and 1395 and was enlarged at the west end in the mid-fifteenth century by two further bays in box timber construction. The west wing was erected around 1490.

Let us go inside into the courtyard with its great lead cistern. On the left is the east wing which was rebuilt around 1632 but was originally built to house the chantry priests who ministered to the Gild of Corpus Christi. On the south side the brick-built house seems to be completely out of character: there used to be a timber kitchen wing here but it was replaced by a house for Leicester's first Chief Constable, Sir Frederick Goodyer, when the town's police force was first formed in 1836. At the same time cells and a charge-room were made on the ground floor of the east wing. Visitors used to be encouraged to press a light switch and to peep through one of the little inspection windows and get a shock when they see a dishevelled prisoner (a dummy) lying on a rough bed! A gibbet which used to be displayed was last used in 1832 when the body of James Cook, hanged for a particularly gruesome murder, was put into it and suspended from a 33ft. pole at the junction of Saffron Lane and Aylestone Road: the object was to prevent it being stolen for dissection for medical research purposes. In the two days that it was displayed 20,000 people went to see it. When he learned of the gibbeting Joseph Foulkes Winks, a Baptist minister, went to the site and continued to preach on the spot until the body was taken down and as a result brought about the end of gibbeting in England. To his wife's annoyance he was thereafter known as 'Gibbet Winks'!

The Guildhall's Great Hall is most impressive with the great curved cruck timbers supporting the roof. It used to have an earthern floor with an open fire in the centre, the smoke finding its way out through the roof. It was here that Common Halls were held, these were the meetings of the 24 Jurats and the 48 ordinary members of the Borough Corporation - usually referred to as 'the twenty-four' and 'the forty eight'. At the west end of the hall is a stand for the town mace, dated 1586, bearing the letters E.R. (Elizabeth Regina) and the initials of the two Chamberlains in office at that time - George Oldham and Thomas Chettle. There are hooks on the roof timbers from which curtains were hung when itinerant companies of players were performing; it is possible that Shakespeare played here. Painted on the ceilings are the seventeenth century arms of the Borough and those of the Hastings family (the Earls of Huntingdon). The arms of Queen Anne hang in the centre of the hall.

The Borough Corporation was an oligarchy - an Act of Parliament in 1489 placed it on a self-elected basis until the Municipal Reform Act was passed in 1835. Only four of the original members survived the first election and the newly elected body showed their displeasure at what had gone on before by auctioning all the town's silver. The sale, at the Town Hall, lasted six days and even the Great Mace was sold. This made £85 and was bought by Mrs. Laughton, the landlady of the George III inn in Wharf Street. It had a chequered history but was eventually bought back by public subscription for the original selling price.

The balcony at the east end of the main hall came from the New Gainsborough in the Market Place, when it was demolished in 1850 to make way for the present Corn Exchange. Going up the stairs, which are modern, into the upper floor of the east wing, we see the Recorder's bedroom on the left. Letters Patent of Edward IV in 1464 separated the Borough Quarter Sessions from those of the County (which were held at the Castle) and appointed the Mayor and four Jurats who had most recently served in that office, together with the Recorder - one learned in the law, who duty was to give legal advice - to be Justices of the Peace within the Borough and to be elected by the Common Hall each year on 21st September. When he was on circuit the Recorder would sleep in this bedroom which has been furnished in the style of the period. The books in the library on this floor are mainly theological and ecclesiastical and are in Latin, Greek and Hebrew: the library is the third oldest in the country. (There are older ones at Bristol and Norwich). It is recorded that the books were kept beneath the tower of St. Martin's Church in 1587 and were moved to the Guildhall in 1632. The massive Beaumanor Chair once stood at the other end of this room; it is made from the base of a huge tree dug up with its roots and inverted forming a seat with five or six roots branching round it: it came from Beaumanor Hall and bears the Arms of the Herrick family.

Now down the stairs again, across the hall and into the west wing. This wing was built as a single lofty room and was divided into three floors in 1563 when the ground floor was made into the Mayor's Parlour. It was panelled in oak in 1637 when the Mayor, Richard Inge, presented the strange looking Mayor's chair. The arms over the chair are those of Charles I: when he was executed they were taken down and hidden; at the Restoration of Charles II in 1660 they were restored. The beautiful overmantel was also installed in the same year; made of oak, it cost £23.0s.0d. - £15.16s.6d. paid to the carver, £4.13s.6d. for wood and the work of one joiner and £2.10s.0d. for colouring and gilding. It was restored to its original colouring in 1954. A great oak refectory table from Exton Hall, made in 1560, with a top made from a single plank 25ft.8ins. long, used to stand in this room. It was removed and returned to Exton in 1991.

The glass of the windows of the Mayor's Parlour was re-set in 1925 with fragments of 15th century painted glass. From the style the artist was almost certainly the same one who painted the glass of Roger Wygston's house. The windows bear the Prince of Wales' feathers, the Royal Crown, the portcullis - emblem of the Tudors, and 'I H S'[1] - the religious symbol. The chalice and wafer, the insignia of the Gild of Corpus Christi, is repeated on all the windows. One window bears the words *'R Lang is a fool 1830'*, scratched with a diamond - there were vandals all those years ago! Portraits of members of the Herrick family and of Sir Thomas White, one of Leicester's benefactors commemorated by a statue on the Clock Tower, hang on the wall.

Over the centuries the Guildhall was the scene of many banquets: one known as the Venison Feast was held annually on 1st August to celebrate the victory over the Spanish Armada. A Mayoral feast in honour of the dedication of St. Martin's Church was an annual highlight; another followed the Annual Mock Hunting of the Hare on Easter Monday. (A dead cat dipped in aniseed water was tied to a horse's tail and trailed from Black Anna's Bower Close on the Dane Hills by a circuitous route back to the Town Hall. A pack of hounds followed by all the civic dignitaries followed the trail and the day ended with a feast). The courtyard was used as a kitchen for cooking the feasts and bear-baiting was arranged for the amusement of the guests: this took place during the 'Interlude' - the interval between the feast and the dessert. The company adjourned to the 'bear garden', a piece of ground for which the annual rent was 20d. A bear was chained to a post and five or six mastiffs were let loose on him: if the bear was disabled another was brought in and on one recorded occasion as many as thirteen appeared in succession. Records show payments of 4s. made 'to two bearwards at Mr. Mayor's dinner' in 1580. Bulls were also baited but there are no references to them in the town accounts. In 1467 it was laid down that no butcher should kill a bull before it had been baited or he would forfeit the carcass, so ensuring a regular supply of bulls for baiting with no expense to the town.

Saltpetre men were appointed during the reign of Elizabeth I to roam the country searching for potassium nitrate (saltpetre) for use in making gunpowder. They had authority to impound any materials from which it could be obtained. Earthen floors were strewn with rushes and food that was dropped was left to decay, ultimately producing saltpetre, and because the saltpetre men had a habit of breaking up floors, a visit from them was regarded with apprehension. There are many entries in the Chamberlains' accounts relating to damage done to the Town Hall by these men: serious settlements in older parts of the buildings may be due to their activities. In 1584 the floor of the kitchen was dug up and in 1588 the Borough paid 4s.

4d. for re-making the earthen floors at the hall. The last reference to a saltpetre man is in an account for 1627-28, when 2s. 2d. was paid for levelling the Town Hall floor after he had dug it up. These men were very high-handed and this caused their office to be abolished during the Commonwealth.

The building of the new Town Hall was completed in 1876 and on 7th August the Mayor, Alderman William Barfoot, led a procession of civic dignitaries from the Old Town Hall to the new one. A dinner at the Corn Exchange was followed by a ball at the Assembly Rooms (now the City Rooms) and a firework display on the Race Course (now Victoria Park).

For the next 46 years the Old Town Hall was little used, except for a town library and by the North Midland School of Cookery - one class was divided from another by curtains loosely hung across the main hall and one of the old prison cells was used as a larder! The school moved to the Domestic Science College in Knighton Fields in 1921. The Hall was in a dilapidated condition and Leicestershire Archaeological and Historical Society played a large part in ensuring its restoration between 1922 and 1926. It was then given the name 'The Guildhall'. On 19th May 1926 the Mayor and Corporation again met there to open it to the public. Since then it has been visited by over one million people. Leicester had been made a City in 1919 and in 1928 the Mayor became Lord Mayor. In 1992-93 the Guildhall was again extensively restored by Leicester City Council.

The pedestrian footway called St. Martin's West separates the Guildhall from **THE CATHEDRAL**. The core of this church is thirteenth century but the exterior was heavily restored between 1844 and 1867. Roman remains were excavated at this time but not preserved. Medieval stone coffins were found and the hammer-beam roof timbers were restored to their original state. The magnificent tower and spire were rebuilt in the 1860s under the direction of Raphael Brandon, the architect. The porch, designed by J. L. Pearson, architect of Truro Cathedral, is a memorial to four members of the Vaughan family, all vicars of St. Martin's - the Reverend E. T. Vaughan and his three sons.

The church is dedicated to St. Martin, a Roman soldier who became a Christian and who, according to tradition, shared his cloak with a beggar. When the Leicester diocese was re-created in 1926 there was some debate concerning whether St. Margaret's or St. Martin's should become the Cathedral. The latter was chosen for it had always been the civic church. The first bishop of the restored diocese was Dr. Cyril Bardsley.

Records of visits by George VI, Elizabeth II and Princess Margaret are displayed. Charles I is also said to have visited the church, but there is no tangible record - perhaps because his wife was a Roman Catholic? An incised slab in the floor of the chancel commemorates Richard III, slain at Bosworth Field.

The church has a double south aisle - the outer aisle was the chapel of the

Gild of Corpus Christi. The Gild of St. George had a meeting place nearby in Guildhall Lane. The Gild's chapel in St. Martin's Church was on the left of the south door, nowadays it houses memorials and colours of the Leicestershire Regiment (the Tigers) from 1688, and books record the names of the fallen, many of whom died from cholera. In days gone by a life-size, armour-clad figure of St. George on horseback stood on a raised platform near the altar in the chapel. On the Gild's feast day the figure was taken out of the church and borne on a wheeled stage through the principal streets, accompanied by the dragon and other characters of the legend, to shouts of 'St. George for England'. This was called 'Riding the George' and was regarded as the greatest holiday of the year - a day devoted to feasting and rejoicing. In 1547, after the Reformation, the horse was sold for 12d. and the custom was abolished.

The oldest memorial in the Cathedral is a slab, six inches thick and weighing 35 cwt. It has been used as a memorial five times - from a priest in the fifteenth century to a Mary Jordan in 1701. The Herrick chapel contains many tombs of the Herrick family. There is a memorial to Alderman Gabriel Newton's son George which also commemorates the founding of his school - 'to clothe 35 poor boys, put them out to trade and educate them rightly' and another to John Johnson the architect who designed the City Rooms and built the Consanguinitarium[2] in Southgate Street in 1792. It was a row of five dwellings in gothic style for his poor relations.

The churchyard was reconstructed a few years ago and beautified by a fountain. Among the gravestones are some to Aldermen, Mayors and an exciseman, but perhaps the most interesting is one to John Fenton who was killed in 1778 by a Frenchman. The murderer was found guilty but pardoned and the inscription criticises the course of justice. It reads:

> *ENQUIRING MORTAL where'er thou art ponder here upon an incident which highly concerns all the progeny of ADAM. Near this place lieth the body of JOHN FENTON who fell by violence May 17th 1778 And remains a sad example of the incompetency of Juridical Institutions to punish a Murderer! He left to mourn this untimely fate a mother, a widow and two children. These but not these alone are greatly injured. Personal security received a mortal wound when vengeance was averted.*

James Fenton, brother of the deceased, had a quarrel with Francis Soules who owed him 6s. after a game of billiards and when Soules produced a pair of loaded pistols James fled to The Green Dragon Inn in the Market Place. Soules came in search of him and in the fracas that ensued John Fenton (the deceased) was shot. Soules was arrested when he took refuge in a garret closet at the Three Crowns Inn. A verdict of wilful murder was brought in at the inquest but when Soules was tried at the Guildhall he was found guilty of the lesser offence of manslaughter. It was this verdict that caused John Fenton's family to be so embittered.

Further along St. Martin's West on the right hand side in the playground of the Grammar School, is the site of **WYGGESTON'S HOSPITAL**, founded by William Wyggeston in 1513. He was a wealthy wool merchant who exported wool to the Flemish weavers through the port of Calais - a staple port through which all such exports had to pass to enable duty (a part of the king's income) to be levied.

William was four times Mayor of Calais, then an English possession, and twice Mayor of Leicester.

He founded his hospital for twelve poor men and twelve poor women who were to be 'blind, lame, decrepit, paralytic or maimed of their limbs, or idiots wanting their natural senses, so that they be peaceable, not disturbing the hospital'. The chapel was dedicated to St. Ursula and for a time the hospital was known as 'St. Ursula's Hospital'. He richly endowed it with lands in various parts of the Midlands. It was built in stone and was demolished in 1875 when the establishment was moved to Hinckley Road where it has since been rebuilt again. A bronze plaque on the corner pillar of the school yard boundary fence tells of the hospital's removal.

We turn left now into **PEACOCK LANE** which was given this name in the eighteenth century from a piece of land called 'The Peacocke': there used to be a Peacock Inn - which probably took its name from the crest of the Manners family - on the corner of Southgate Street. In earlier years it was called St. Francis Lane from its proximity to the Greyfriars Franciscan Friary.

As we walk along Peacock Lane we come to **NEW STREET** on the right. This street was laid out in 1711 when the Herrick estate on the site of the Greyfriars Friary was broken up and purchased by the Ruding family of Westcotes. The street cuts right through the old friary area and was given its name because it was the first street in which bricks were used for domestic buildings. Prior to that date all houses in Leicester were constructed of timber with wattle and daub infillings. Most of the buildings are original, built with the narrow bricks typical of the eighteenth century: its now a street of accountants and solicitors.

If we walk up New Street for a few yards and turn round we get a splendid view of the tower and spire of the Cathedral. Pausing and facing the iron railings of the car park, on our left used to stand an ancient pump over a well: four of the houses nearby used to pay an annual rent of one shilling to the Borough Corporation for its use. Looking diagonally across the car park on the right we see a fragment of stone wall - the last remaining relic of the Greyfriars Friary. Richard III's body was put into a stone coffin and interred in the chapel of the friary and in 1495 Henry VII erected an alabaster tomb over it complete with effigy - at a cost of £10.1s. With the Reformation and the dissolution of the friary early in the next century, the buildings were demolished and the tomb broken up: the stone coffin was used as a horse trough in the stable yard of the White Horse Inn in Gallowtree Gate for many years afterwards.

Returning to Peacock Lane we go forward into St. Martin's passing on the right the third Alderman Newton's school of 1864, build in red brick faced with stone and decorated at eaves level with stone carvings which remind one of the Queen's Beasts. It accommodated 100 pupils and has since been enlarged by a wing built at right angles to the original school: it is now occupied by the private Leicester Grammar School. A few yards further on is the superb National Westminster Bank premises, built in whitish stone in 1900. The two pavilion-like structures on its roof are reminiscent of the government buildings in New Dehli designed by Sir Edwin Lutyens. This bank used to be Pares' Bank, then Parr's Bank followed by the National Provincial Bank.

Now we turn left into **ST. MARTINS EAST**, past the Provost's house and the diocesan offices and at number 5a we have a view of one of the few private gardens in the City centre. This house, built by architects Stockdale Harrison for their practice, is known as 'Architects' Cottage'. The east end of the Cathedral is on the left as we go back into Guildhall Lane.

We turn right and proceed to the corner of Silver Street and Carts Lane to **THE GLOBE** public house, which has two windows which were bricked up to save window tax levied in the 1790s. In 1880 nineteen different carriers ran regular services from various Leicestershire villages to Leicester and made the Globe their stopping place while they purchased supplies for their customers. There is said to be a well 160ft. deep which supplied water for brewing beneath the floor of one of the public rooms. Silversmiths used to have their shops in Silver Street - it has borne this name since at least 1587. Loseby Lane on the opposite corner, takes its name from Henry de Loseby who owned land here in the fourteenth century. Its alternative name was Pig Lane when the pig market was moved here in the eighteenth century. On the right of Loseby Lane stands the **CROWN AND THISTLE** public house. This is said to be the only licensed premises that the Lord Mayor can enter wearing the chain of office. The Lord Mayor goes there every year on the feast of St. John the Baptist, 24th June, to collect the peppercorn rent - a damask rose and four old pennies. The custom goes back to 24th February 1636 when the site was sold to James Teale, a shoemaker, and his wife Elizabeth, by the Duchy of Lancaster for 40s. The red damask rose is the insignia of the Duchy. The Hostel of St. Mary of Newarke, which was endowed by Henry, the first Duke of Lancaster, used to stand here. The public house used to be called the 'Star and Ball': it was re-named in honour of the unification of England and Scotland in 1707 - the crown of England with the thistle of Scotland. There is a legend that there is an underground passage from the premises to the Cathedral at the rear.

CARTS LANE is named after Dr. Samuel Carte, son of a clothier of

Coventry. He was vicar of St. Martin's Church from 1700 to 1740 when he died aged 87. On the corner of Carts Lane and **HIGH STREET** is what used to be Butler's chemist shop. Its High Street frontage is an interesting relic from the recent past with its façade panelled with coloured tiles. At the upper level a chemist stands flanked by large stoppered jars filled with coloured liquids so beloved by pharmacists of years gone by. The front of his counter bears the legend 'Chemists by Examination' and below is a ship in full sail, each sail bearing one word of the inscription 'Sea Breeze Saline'. Across the sky is the message 'For headache drink **SEA BREEZE**' and a life buoy floats on the sea bearing the words 'Saves Life'.

The present High Street was known as Swinesmarket until the late sixteenth century. In 1524 the sale of pigs was moved to Parchment Lane, so-called because parchment was made there - it later became New Bond Street. Parchment Lane itself acquired the name Swinesmarket after 1594 and retained it long after the pig market had been moved to Loseby Lane.

When the **SHIRES** shopping precinct was built the façade of the former Leicestershire Co-operative store was retained and the rear was demolished. Debenham's store on the St. Peter's Lane side of the development was opened in the autumn of 1991 and the remainder was finished in 1992. The High Street end of New Bond Street was incorporated into the precinct as one of its principal entrances near to the Clock Tower. Before the Shires was built extensive archaeological excavations took place revealing many interesting features, including a Roman cellar, ancient rubbish pits, privies, cess pits and middens. The numerous artifacts found gave clues to the way of life. This shopping precinct promises to bring back prosperity to High Street after a period of decline.

The medieval **EAST GATE**, (and probably the Roman one too), spanned the road opposite New Bond Street, hence the name, East Gates - the short street at the bottom end of High Street. The gate was too narrow and too low for farm carts to pass through so, along with the other three gates, it was sold by auction for building material at the Three Crowns Inn on 21st March 1774; it had to be carted away within six weeks. A Blue Plaque marks the site.

LORD'S PLACE, a town mansion built round three or all four sides of a square, used to stand on the north side of High Street. Erected in the sixteenth century in the reign of Queen Elizabeth I by Richard Reynold, it was at first known as Reynold's Place. His son Nicholas sold it to Henry, the third Earl of Huntingdon in 1569 when it was called Lord's Place. Mary Queen of Scots stayed there in November of that year when being taken from Tutbury to Coventry. Other visitors were James I in 1612 and Charles I in 1642. The mansion changed hands several times and was partly demolished around 1702 and only a tower, built in brick which stood in about the middle of the front wall of the old mansion, remained and became known as the Huntingdon Tower. It was pulled down in 1902 when High

Street was widened ready for the coming of the new electric trams. A plaque, bearing an impression of the Tower and an inscription (which is not quite accurate) attached to the present Huntingdon Tower Buildings, commemorates the site of Lord's Place.

As we walk up High Street towards its junction with Highcross Street the **SINGER BUILDING** is on our left. Look at it closely for it depicts the 'Age of Imperialism'. There is a kangaroo for Australia, a camel for Egypt, a polar bear for Canada, a tiger for India, an elephant for Burma and an ostrich for South Africa. This was the Leicester headquarters of the Singer Sewing Machine Company. Built in 1902 and designed by Arthur Wakerley, it celebrated the Coronation of Edward VII which had been delayed when he underwent the first operation for appendicitis. A few doors further on is what used to be well known as the **'FAMILY FRYPAN'** - a hardware business founded in 1862 by William Hallam and distinguished by the enormous frying pan hanging above the shop front. The original building was demolished when High Street was widened around 1900 and the business was closed down in July 1989. The premises are now used as a betting shop.

We turn right into **HIGHCROSS STREET** and notice a cross of granite setts in the roadway which marks the site of the last remaining pillar of the old **HIGH CROSS**. A Wednesday market was held here from the twelfth century for the sale of butter, poultry, eggs, fruit and vegetables and in the late fourteenth century a Friday market was held on the same site at which bread was sold in addition to country produce. To provide some shelter a market consisting of eight stone pillars, set in a circle, supporting a pointed roof, was built in 1577 at a cost of nearly £100. The Horse and Trumpet Inn

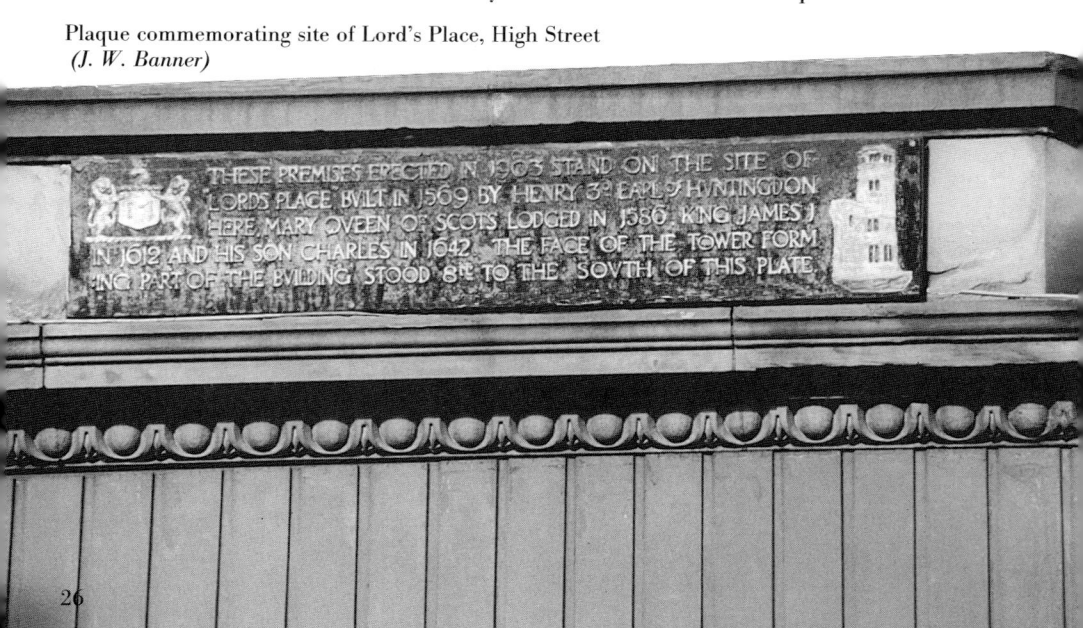

Plaque commemorating site of Lord's Place, High Street
(J. W. Banner)

Highcross Street c.1830, by John Flower *(Leicester City Council)*

on the corner - landlord around 1750 Alderman Gabriel Newton - had its sign attached to one of the pillars. Country folk would bring their baskets of produce and sit beneath the market to sell it. If they hung any washing between the pillars they were liable to be fined a shilling. The road was very narrow and there was just enough room for carriages to pass. The High Cross became ruinous and it was sold in portions in 1773. Three pillars were bought for the Three Crowns Inn, (on the site of the present National Westminster Bank in Horsefair Street), one was used to support the ceiling and the other two to make a portico. One pillar was retained in situ until 1836: it too became an impediment to traffic so it was taken down and the Wednesday Market was moved in 1884 to the Saturday Market Place.

Highcross Street used to be called High Street in medieval times; it was the town's principal thoroughfare running between the north and south gates. It was the only street to be paved and for that reason it was literally a 'high street' - the origin of the name 'High Street' for all medieval principal streets.

In 1830 John Flower produced a series of drawings of Leicester as he knew it. Of the buildings shown in his drawings of Highcross Street only two have survived - the shop formerly run by Morgans the locksmiths and the Free Grammar School. Near Morgans' shop is a fragment of wall which was part of the County Gaol - no doubt left to support the neighbouring structure when the prison was demolished in 1837. This prison was built in 1791-2 at a cost of £6,000 and designed by John Johnson who built the Consanguinitarium. The builder was George Moneypenny; he became the first prisoner - for debt!

We pass the end of **FREESCHOOL LANE**; it was given this name in

1573 when the **FREE GRAMMAR SCHOOL** was built on the corner, though before that it was called **DEAD LANE** from the public hangings which took place there. When William Wyggeston died in 1536 he left a fortune; his brother Thomas, a priest, and William's wife Agnes were both executors of his will and they decided to use some of William's money to found a Free Grammar School in 1550. Until 1573 the pupils were taught in the ancient St. Peter's Church. This building however was in a ruinous state and had to be pulled down. As head of the Duchy of Lancaster, Queen Elizabeth sold them the stone for £25 and this was used to build a new school which still stands to this day. Remains of the church foundations were found during archaeological excavations prior to the building of the Shires shopping precinct. In the mid-eighteenth century 300 boys received their education here but by the early nineteenth century numbers had shrunk to fifty day scholars and thirty boarders who lodged in the headmaster's house adjoining. The pupils dwindled to less than half a dozen and it was closed in 1841. The building became a joiner's shop in 1875 and from 1880 to 1936 it was Spurway's carpet warehouse. It used to have five dormer windows but these disappeared when it was re-roofed in 1953.

A name plate on the wall of a building across the road records that this was the site of **BLUE BOAR LANE** - a street which was closed many years ago and incorporated into a factory yard. From the thirteenth to the fifteenth century the 24 Jurats - the senior members of the Borough Corporation - used to hold their meetings or 'morningspeeches' in the old Moot Hall, sometimes referred to as 'The Old Mayor's Hall', which stood in this lane. Later the Moot Hall was divided by a wall and half was used as a coal store and the remainder as a prison.

Daniel Lambert's father was the gaoler of a prison in Blue Boar Lane and Daniel used to help him: he was said to have a very kindly way and would spend hours talking to prisoners in the condemned cell giving them words of comfort and support. He succeeded his father as gaoler but when he became too fat to get down the narrow passages he was retired and given a pension of £50 per year although he was only in his thirties.

The undistinguished building to which the 'Site of Blue Boar Lane' plate is attached is built where the **WHITE BOAR INN** stood in August 1485 and became the **BLUE BOAR** a month or two later. When Richard III came to Leicester on 20th August the Castle was in a ruinous state and he had to stay at an ordinary inn - the White Boar. No doubt the landlord would be highly delighted - he would be able to say 'King Richard slept here'. It would be good for business and of course the white boar was Richard's badge. Unfortunately when the King was slain at Bosworth Field these plans came to nought and the name of the inn was changed to Blue Boar - the badge of the Earl of Oxford, a supporter of Henry Tudor who became Henry VII after his victory at Bosworth.

Richard III did not sleep well in strange beds so it is said that he brought

(Leicester City Council)

OLD BLUE BOAR INN, LEICESTER.

his own bedstead with him to the White Boar and left it there when he set off the following day, no doubt confidently expecting to sleep in it again after he had defeated Henry Tudor. The story goes that the bedstead remained at the Blue Boar and, as part of the fixtures and fittings, was passed down from landlord to landlord until, in 1613, Mistress Clarke, the wife of the landlord thought she might as well make use of it. As she dragged it across the bedchamber a gold coin fell out of its double bottom. She removed one of the bases and found a hoard of gold coins, some of Richard III's reign and some of earlier reigns. She and her husband decided that they would keep their good fortune secret but they soon showed signs of affluence and five years later he became Mayor of Leicester. After he had died and his wife had taken over as landlady, it soon became clear to the inn's staff that she must have hidden wealth and a housemaid plotted with a group of men to rob her. The men stayed at the inn and during the night loaded Mistress Clark's valuables on to their horses. The landlady awoke and, to prevent her from screaming, her gown was thrust into her mouth and she choked to death. The culprits were soon apprehended, tried and found guilty: the housemaid was burned at the stake and the men were hanged - no doubt in public and probably in Dead Lane, today's Freeschool Lane.

The Blue Boar Inn was demolished in 1836 and Leicester lost what would have been a great tourist attraction. Another inn, which was reputed to be haunted, was built on the site soon to be replaced by today's unattractive structure.

Notes on Chapter One
[1] *IHS First three letters of Greek for Jesus; often taken as initials of Jesus Hominum Salvator 'Jesus savior of men'.*
[2] *Consanguinitarium - from the latin consanguineus: related by blood.*

OUT AND ABOUT IN LEICESTER
CHAPTER TWO

ROUTE:
St. Nicholas Circle, Castle Gardens, The Newarke, Castle View, Castle Precincts, The Newarke, Southgates, Friar Lane, Berridge Street, Horsefair Street, Town Hall Square, Horsefair Street.

STARTING PLACE:
Entrance to Castle Gardens near West Bridge.

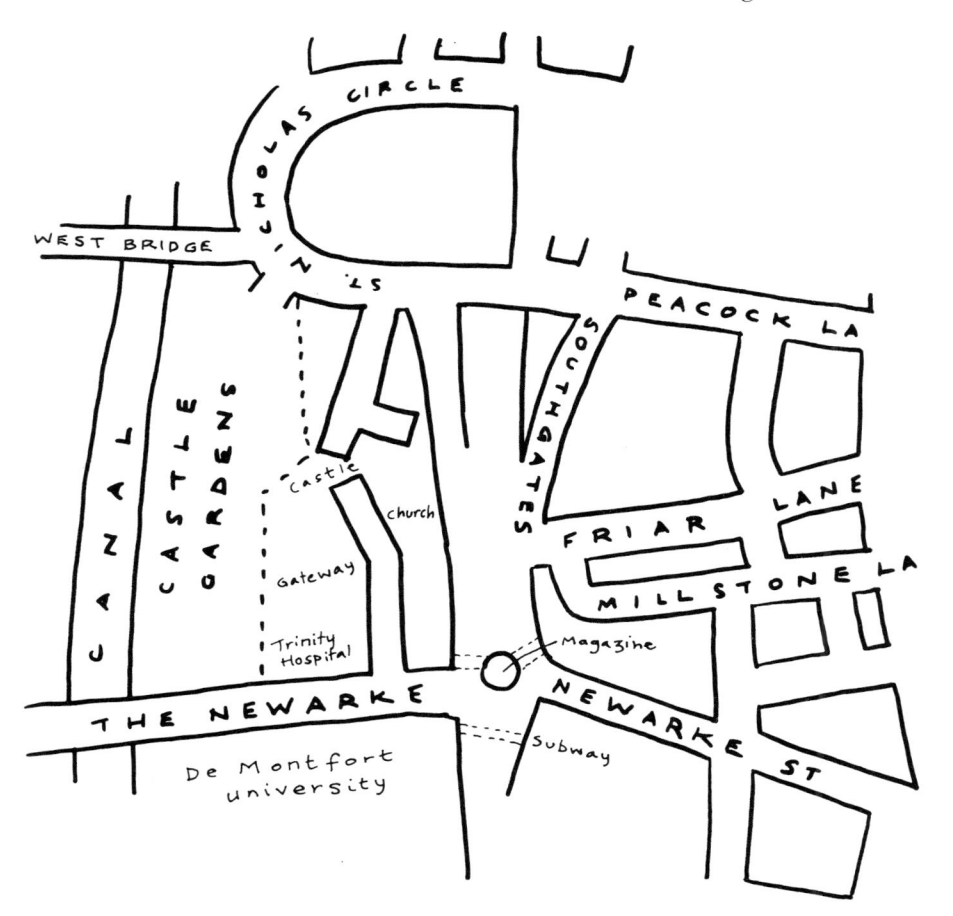

RICHARD III
KING OF ENGLAND
1483 1485

Our second 'arm-chair tour' begins on the city side of West Bridge. As mentioned in our first tour, the area between the bridge and the Holiday Inn used to be called Everard Place and the bronze statue of the fifth Duke of Rutland, at present in the Market Place, stood here for some years following its removal from its earlier site near the Corn Exchange. On the left on the bend in St. Nicholas Circle, near the entrance to Talbot Street, there used to be a large wooden hut which housed Leicester's earliest Labour Exchange.

As we go into the **CASTLE GARDENS** we are entering a beautiful part of the **CASTLE PARK.** The colourful flower beds in spring and summer create a haven of peace and tranquillity. This part of the River Soar, known as the Mile Straight, was canalised in the late nineteenth century and the eight mile stretch of footpaths and cycleway along the river and the Grand Union Canal follows the line of the old Great Central Railway, passing through Castle Park where the old worsted spinning an dyeing factories on the further bank provide an insight into Leicester's early industrial history. Riverboat trips operate from the landing stage during the summer.

On the left is the bronze statue of Richard III with the castle's Great Hall and the crocketed spire of St. Mary de Castro Church forming an impressive backdrop. The castle mound, or motte, clothed by trees in summertime, is a little farther on.

When the Normans built their castles, probably using Saxon labour, they had a great moat excavated and the earth was used to form a motte. A wall or palisade was erected between the moat and mound to form a bailey which enclosed the domestic buildings. Leicester castle mound was thrown up around 1069 and was originally 54 feet high: when 14 feet were removed to make a bowling green around 1840 five skeletons were found, including one of a giant!

Leaving Castle Gardens we enter **THE NEWARKE** and turn left. On the right are the ruined remains of St. Mary's Vicarage and on the left the modern residential accommodation of **TRINITY HOSPITAL**. In 1330 Henry, the third Earl of Lancaster, received a licence authorising him to found a hospital 'to the honour of God and the Virgin Mary' which was confirmed by a Bull issued by Pope John XXII, then resident in Avignon. It was founded in the following year for a warden, four chaplains, fifty poor and infirm folk and five women. Twenty of the poor and infirm were permanent inmates who lived in a house adjoining the hospital chapel: they were chosen from candidates who could plead poverty, blindness or lameness, or were stricken with palsy, had lost a limb or were suffering from some incurable disease. The warden had to pay them a penny a day and supply them with a tunic and hood every Michaelmas. The remaining thirty were temporary inmates - poor folk suffering from passing ailments and asking alms of the hospital in charity: they were housed in the body of the chapel. The five women cared for the inmates and lived in a house next to

Trinity Hospital *(Leicester City Council)*

the chapel and were paid 1½d. per day. If one of them became infirm she was provided for until a place became available as one of the twenty permanent inmates. The priests had a house with a common hall and sleeping apartment.

When Henry Earl of Lancaster died in 1345 his son Henry Plantagenet of Grosmont succeeded him and, as a reward for remarkable military exploits during the Hundred Years War with France, was created Duke of Lancaster. He joined the Teutonic Knights in their crusade against the heathen Lithuanians and was taken prisoner and held to ransom in Prussia. He believed the Duke of Brunswick to be responsible and they agreed to settle their quarrel by a tournament. The king of France intervened and Henry accepted a thorn from a crown of Jesus Christ as an inducement to settle the dispute. From then onwards he vowed to devote himself to the charitable works of his father's hospital and became known as 'the Good Duke'.

In 1351 he was authorised by Edward III to enlarge the hospital. Three years later he provided accommodation for 100 poor men and women, or bedesmen as they were called, with 10 women to care for them, and built the collegiate church of the Annunciation of Our Lady and provided for the maintenance of a dean, 12 canons, 13 vicars, 6 choristers and 3 clerks. (The clergy of collegiate churches relied on the church for their stipends and officiated at all church services. They were some of the few educated people and did other unpaid work, possibly concerning local government, during the remainder of the week). The Holy Thorn was preserved in the church which stood where the Hawthorn Building of De Montfort University on our right, stands today - there are still two arches, all that remains of the church, in the basement. The area where the enlarged hospital and church stood was enclosed by a wall and called 'The New Work' - since corrupted to 'The Newarke'.

The Good Duke died of plague in 1361 and was interred in his new church. King Edward III, Queen Philippa, Edward the Black Prince and all the nobility attended his funeral. He had no sons and the honor of Leicester was divided between his two daughters, Maud and Blanche, but when Maud and her husband William, Duke of Bavaria, also died of plague, Blanche, wife of John of Gaunt, the third son of Edward III, inherited the whole and her husband assumed the title of Duke of Lancaster.

The hospital ran smoothly until the first half of the sixteenth century when it was disrupted by the Reformation and all collegiate establishments were abolished under the Chantries Act of 1547. The beautiful church of the Annunciation of Our Lady was destroyed and with it the tombs of the Good Duke and other notable citizens. The hospital with its original chapel survived as Trinity Hospital. The residential buildings have been rebuilt several times and up to 40 residents can now be accommodated.

It is possible to visit the hospital by arrangement. The great arches in the entrance lobby survive from the earliest building. In a glass case on the wall 'Queen Elizabeth's Pocket Piece' is displayed. This is a nutmeg grater with room for about a dozen nutmegs. Made of oak it bears the date 1519 and has inscriptions carved on each of its four sides such as *'flee idleness and be wel occupied'*; *'think wel and say wel, but rather do wel'*; and *'This belongeth to the Old Ospital in Leicester'*. A great bronze vessel known as 'John of Gaunt's Porridge Pot' stands in the corner. It holds 61 gallons and was originally used to prepare frumenty for sale to the populace. (Frumenty was made by boiling whole grains of wheat with milk and sugar and was a forerunner of breakfast cereals). The pot was later used for cooking pottage for the hospital inmates and when a great banquet for veterans of the Crimean War was held at the Corn Exchange in 1877 it was borrowed to cook 66 plum puddings.

In the chapel are six panels listing the many benefactors of the hospital headed by Henry of Grosmont, Duke of Lancaster, though his father was the founder. To the left of the altar is the tomb with an effigy of Lady Mary Hervey, a member of the Castle household. Portraits of Henry, third Earl of Lancaster, the founder, and his son Henry, first Duke of Lancaster, the Good Duke, hang in the common room.

We turn left into Castle View and the building of random stone on the right is William Wyggeston's **CHANTRY HOUSE** which he built in 1512 to house two chantry priests whose duty was to say mass for his soul and to care for his tomb after his death. He died in 1536 and his body was laid to rest in a tomb in the Church of the Annunciation of Our Lady in the Newarke, only to be destroyed along with the church in 1547. The Chantry House now forms part of the Newarke Houses Museum.

Ahead is the **TURRET GATEWAY**, built in 1422, one of the two entrances into the Castle precincts. Leicester people usually refer to it as 'Rupert's Gateway' no doubt because Prince Rupert of the Rhine, the nephew of Charles I, was the Commander of the Royalist forces during the Civil War. (Rupert's sister Sophia, married the Elector of Hanover and their son became King George I). Though the citizens of Leicester initially tried to adopt a neutral attitude, they tended to support the Parliamentarians when Rupert demanded £2,000 from the Borough Corporation in 1642. Though his request was countermanded by the King in a letter written in September of that year, £500 which had been sent in the interim was never repaid.

Three years later on 25th May 1645 the King decided to attack the town with an army of 6,000 men facing a total of around 2,000 defenders. All the shops were closed and the defences were strengthened as far as possible. Prince Rupert located his cannon on the earthworks of the Raw Dykes - the Roman aqueduct, part of which still survives - near to the site of the present Royal Infirmary. He bombarded the town inflicting great damage and causing many casualties; both the Chantry House and the Turret Gateway were severely damaged. The latter was damaged even more in an election riot in 1832.

The Turret Gateway has associations with the legend of Black Anna. The story goes that she lived in a cave which she had scratched out with her fingernails in the Danehills area to the west of the city. She would hide in a pollard oak which overhung the mouth of the cave and watch for children passing. She would seize one, suck its blood and hang out its skin to dry. It was said that if she was unable to catch a child she would run wailing up and down an underground passage from the cave to the Turret Gateway. Sometimes she would sit in one of the rooms over the arch of the gateway waiting for the opportunity to grab children as they passed through. Far-fetched as this legend sounds, it may have foundation on fact, for in pagan times the druids used to sacrifice children to Danu, or Anna, the wife of Ludd, the Sky God, to ensure fertility. Even today elderly people recall how they had to pass through the Turret Gateway on their way to and from school and how they would run like the wind in case they should encounter Black Anna!

As we walk along Castle View, the garden of the Newarke Houses Museum is on the right with many interesting relics from the past including the gates from Quenby Hall - a superb example of the blacksmith's skill. In the 1850s the Squire of Quenby Hall, a member of the Ashby family, presented these ornamental gates to be erected at Leicester's Infirmary. On the other side of the road is an attractive herb garden and the tower and spire of St. Mary de Castro Church dominate the view straight ahead with a glimpse of the castle to the left.

Visitors expecting all castles to be like those of Edward I in North Wales, with great towers and curtain walls, might be excused if they are a little disappointed when they see **LEICESTER CASTLE** for the first time.

Turret Gateway and St. Mary De Castro Church from Castle View *(Leicester City Council)*

Unlike King Edward's, Norman castles consisted of a motte, a moat and a bailey which enclosed the living quarters and Leicester's castle followed this pattern. To allow time for the freshly dug soil to settle it is thought that the original castle was built of wood on top of the motte around 1069 but no trace of it remained when the top 14 feet was removed in 1840 nor was there any trace of stone foundations - they had probably been robbed out for use elsewhere. The first stone structure was built by Henry II in the middle of the twelfth century. His son, also Henry, known as the 'Young King', (he was crowned in his father's lifetime to ensure the succession, but died before his father), rebelled against the Crown and was supported by Robert 'Blanchmains', third Earl of Leicester. The rebellion was put down and to punish the Earl the King dismantled the Castle in 1173, except for the Great Hall and kitchen, much of which still survives. It is said to be the oldest domestic building north of the Alps. The Castle eventually passed into the hands of Henry Bolingbroke, Duke of Lancaster, who became King Henry IV in 1399 when his cousin, Richard II was deposed and murdered. Because he then lived at Westminster, the castle with no resident Earl, fell into disrepair. It became so ruinous that much of it was pulled down and sold for building material in 1633. In 1695 it was decided to restore the hall and the outer walls were rebuilt with bricks burnt in a kiln in Welford Place. Inside much of the structure of the Great Hall remains. The castle was dedicated as a Court of Justice in 1274 by Edmund Crouchback, Earl of Leicester, when he held the first Assizes, and it has continued as a court until very recently. In earlier days, if a prisoner was found guilty he was liable to be summarily executed on Castle Green.

Originally the hall had aisles - rows of wooden pillars helping to support the roof. In 1821 the pillars were taken down and the Hall divided to form magistrates courts. The Castle was purchased by the Leicestershire Justices from the Duchy of Lancaster in 1875 and ownership was transferred to Leicestershire County Council on its formation in 1889. With the building of new courts in Pocklington's Walk, the future of the Castle is uncertain.

The suite of rooms which accommodated the Earl and his family have almost entirely disappeared: only one of the service rooms known as **JOHN OF GAUNT'S CELLAR** survives. After the Dukes of Lancaster became Kings of England the Castle served as the estate office for the Duchy of Lancaster's Leicestershire estates and a place for holding Courts of Assize.

The **TUDOR GATEHOUSE**, rebuilt in 1445 after a fire, is the second entrance to the castle precincts. It is sometimes referred to as 'John of Gaunt's Cottage' but this probably alludes to the original structure for he died 46 years before the present gatehouse was built. It used to adjoin the church but part was demolished in 1848 because it was thought wrong that people might be sleeping next to where Holy Communion was being celebrated.

Like many timber-built structures the gatehouse is jettied - the upper floor

Tudor Gatehouse *(Leicester City Council)*

overhangs the ground floor. This is a device whereby the weight of the upper section of the building is carried by the ends of the floor beams and by a cantilever principle, takes weight off the centre of the floor. In the seventeenth century the Tudor Gatehouse was incorporated into the timber and brick Castle House next door and in the Georgian period a further house was added on the north. These houses are now used as lodgings for High Court Judges on circuit and distinguished guests of the County Council.

Parliament has met in Leicester three times, twice at the Castle. In 1414 one of the Houses assembled in the large hall of the Greyfriars Friary and the other met in a house in Redcross Street. The session was concerned with the abolition of Lollardy - a heresy propagated by John Wycliffe and his followers. The Lollards wanted the Bible to be translated into English so that it could be read by everyone: they also disagreed with certain Catholic dogmas such as [1]transubstantiation and were critical of the wealth of the Church. Heretics were punished by burning at the stake and had their property confiscated. For this reason the session was termed the 'Fire and Faggot Parliament'. In 1426 the second Leicester Parliament was held in the Great Hall of the Castle and became known as the 'Parliament of Bats'. Because of a feud between the Duke of Gloucester, youngest brother of Henry V, and Cardinal Henry Beaufort, Bishop of Winchester and Lord Chancellor, the carrying of weapons was strictly forbidden. Barons supporting either side concealed clubs or 'bats' in their clothes and loaded their pouch-like sleeves with stones. Fortunately neutral members succeeded in placating the two parties before they came to blows. Unhealthy conditions prevailing in Westminster caused Parliament to come to Leicester for the third time in 1450.

The **CHURCH OF ST. MARY DE CASTRO** (St. Mary of the Castle), faces the Castle across Castle Green. It is thought that a Saxon church stood on the site but no trace of it remains. The present church was founded in 1107 by Robert de Beaumont, the first Earl of Leicester, as the chapel for his castle. Members of the royal family and other important guests frequently stayed here and the original church proved to be too small and was extended by the beautiful long chancel built in typical Norman style in 1160. At this time it became a collegiate church administered by a dean and twelve canons.

Early in the thirteenth century a small south aisle was built, but in the second half of that century the church was found to be too small for the parishioners to worship there, the south aisle was demolished and what was virtually a second church, dedicated to the Holy Trinity, was built alongside the original church of St. Mary during the earldom of Simon de Montfort. Arcades were later cut in the dividing wall making the two churches into one, with a nave and an enormous south aisle, bigger than the nave, 32 feet wide. When this second south aisle was built it was impossible to build the tower and spire outside the church as is usual because there was insufficient space on Castle Green, so it had to be built internally. A north aisle was built in 1543, but it fell down in 1667 and the existing north aisle wall is comparatively modern except for the Norman doorway. There is another disused Norman doorway at the west end of this aisle which would appear to have been moved from the west end of the nave at some time.

In addition to being open for its services the church opens to the public on Saturday afternoons in summer. Let us go inside and look round. The walls are very dark but are steeped in history. In the chancel is a set of three Norman sedilia said to be one of the finest in the country. Notice the lancet windows of the nave's clerestory - those on the north side still fulfil their original function, admitting light, but those on the south sides are now contained within the church. These are part of the earliest church, more of which remains below the west window of the nave.

There is a second fine set of sedilia and a piscina in the south aisle. On the floor near the font, beneath the tower, are some medieval floor tiles; this area serves as a baptistry. Notice the metal staple on the rim of the font and its wooden lid: in medieval times it was the custom to bless water for baptisms once a year and to leave it in the font; at the Council of Lyons in 1230 Pope Benedict X issued a decree ordaining that all fonts should be fitted with covers; the decree was promulgated in England by Edmund Rich, Archbishop of Canterbury, in 1236. A staple enabled the cover to be secured by a locking device preventing Holy Water from being stolen for purposes of black magic.

John of Gaunt, Earl of Leicester and Duke of Lancaster, lived and died at Leicester Castle. During the Peasants' Revolt in 1381, fearing an attack by a mob from London, he had his valuables loaded on to carts and taken to Leicester Abbey: fearing for his own safety, the Abbot refused them and they were stored in St. Mary de Castro Church. John was a patron of Geoffrey Chaucer who married Philippa Roët, sister of Catherine Swynford, John's third wife, in this church.

During the 1426 meeting of Parliament at the Castle the five year old Henry VI was knighted in St. Mary's along with forty other candidates. After the ceremony their horses were brought into the church, the new knights mounted and rode them down the aisle and into Castle Yard where they showered money among the assembled crowd amid cries of 'largesse, largesse'.

Outside, at eaves level, each side of the chancel has a row of grotesque corbel heads, some human, others representing animals. In the fourteenth century the church had a slender broach spire: this was destroyed by lightning in 1783 and replaced by a crocketed one added to the earlier tower. This spire was much repaired and shortened twice and is now 179 feet high. The pinnacles and battlements were added to the tower by Sir George Gilbert Scott in Victorian times. We are told that over a hundred years ago acrobats used to perform by sliding down a rope fastened to the top of the spire and stretched across Castle Green.

On a warm sunny day a pleasant hour can be spent in the churchyard studying the Swithland slate gravestones, most of which bear the names of monumental masons, and it is interesting to follow and compare their work and admire their beautiful carving and calligraphy. The medieval wall between the graveyard and the

St. Mary de Castro Church *(Leicester City Council)*

garden of the Newarke Houses Museum has fifty or sixty circular holes of about nine inches diameter cut through it. It is said that weapons were fired through them at the Royalist forces during the Siege of Leicester in the Civil War.

Look at the stonework of the tower and note how steeply the roof used to slope when it was slated. When lead began to be used for roofing it was found that a more gentle pitch was needed and in this case the point of the roof was lowered considerably.

Both the Castle precinct and the Newarke were enclosed areas, within which the Duchy of Lancaster had reserved certain rights to itself excluding the burgesses from any jurisdiction here.

We now return to **THE NEWARKE** reflecting that the reason Richard III had to stay at an ordinary inn in 1485 was because the Castle was in a ruinous state, and the two arches remaining from the Church of the Annunciation of Our Lady, in the basement of the Hawthorn Building (the former College of Art and Technology), remind us that his body was laid in state here for two days before interment in the Greyfriars Friary chapel.

A bronze plaque mounted on the corner pillar of the fence surrounding the Hawthorn Building is a reminder of days gone by when a fair was held here every Shrove Tuesday, at which oranges, ginger bread and similar delicacies were sold. At two o'clock a bell was rung and all those who had no taste for horseplay would either withdraw from the Newarke or protect their legs with straw or other padding. A group of wagonners known as the 'Whipping Toms' appeared armed with wagon whips which they claimed the right to use on all who remained in the fairground unless they paid them money (usually 2d.) to escape molestation. Their favourite practice was to form two lines, thrust a victim between them and whip him up and down the row. In theory they were forbidden to whip anyone above the knee but this rule was frequently violated and, in consequence, a savage brawl often developed. As a result the custom was abolished by the Leicester Improvement Act of 1846. The plaque states:

> *'The Whipping Toms. On this spot stood the Whipping Toms who on Shrove Tuesday, in accordance with the Ancient Custom, armed themselves with wagon whips and flogged anyone who entered the precincts of the Newarke. The sport was abolished by Act of Parliament in 1846'.*

Next to the Hawthorn Building there used to be a nineteenth century barrack square which was demolished when the Newarke pedestrian underpass was constructed. The square was surrounded by military housing and the high-rise James Went Building of the De Montfort University occupies the site today. The Reverend Canon James Went was headmaster of the Wyggeston Boys' School for 42 years until 1919 when the school moved to its new site next to Victoria Park.

When Henry, Duke of Lancaster, enlarged his hospital in 1354 he enclosed the area with a wall and, apart from the Turret Gateway from the castle precinct, the only entrance into the New Work from outside the town was through the **MAGAZINE GATEWAY**, a town gate in miniature, which stands straight before us. At first the gateway was used as a prison - scratchings made by prisoners can be seen on the walls. It is said that criminals found guilty and condemned to death were sometimes hanged here. A platform with a scaffold attached was erected over the arch on the Newarke Street side of the gateway: prisoners were brought out through the large window and a priest administered the last rites through the smaller window next to it. (Was this why Newarke Street used to be called Hangman's Lane?).

Soon after 1600 the gateway was acquired by the Borough and became known as The Magazine when that authority stored armaments and weapons here from 1642. This was the time of the Civil War and many members of the Leicester Parliamentary Committee had their homes in The Newarke and were anxious to keep an eye on the whereabouts of their means of defence.

All wheeled traffic went through the Magazine arch until 1905 when a road was constructed to one side; pedestrians still went through until 1968. Alterations aimed at improving the flow of traffic left the Magazine Gateway isolated on an island which could only be reached from the newly created pedestrian underpass.

Since 1971 the gateway has been the museum of the Royal Leicestershire Regiment - the Tigers. The flag flown beside the Union Flag is the regiment's own; its colours, red, black and pearl grey, are taken from the red coat, black hat and pearl grey piping of past uniforms. The number XVII in the centre indicates that it was the 17th Regiment of Foot. The title 'Leicestershire' was assumed in 1772; 'Royal' was incorporated into the name after World War II. The two cannons on the Newarke Street side were taken at Sebastopol during the Crimean War.

With William Wyggeston's Chantry House, which we passed on our way to the Castle, **SKEFFINGTON HOUSE** forms the Newarke Houses Museum. This fine house with its three-gabled front, built in 1610, was the town house of the Skeffington family of Skeffington Hall. It is almost the sole survivor of the large houses which used to fill the Newarke from the sixteenth to the nineteenth centuries: here the wealthy people of the town lived very much a law unto themselves, exempt from paying rates to the borough and from the authority of the borough magistrates. The house at one time housed the Wyggeston Girls' School and later the Gateway Boys' School. Both these buildings were damaged in the Siege of Leicester and again in an air raid in World War II.

The **NEWARKE HOUSES MUSEUM** has exhibits relating to the

CONSANGUINITARIUM, AT LEICESTER.
With Four Houses in front, built by the Founder on his place of his Birth.

social history of the city and county. Among them are reminders of Daniel Lambert including his huge chair, walking stick, a suit of clothes and a portrait. He was born in 1770 and was quite normal until he was nineteen when he began to put on weight: he was 5ft. 11ins. tall, weighed 52st. 11lb., was 9ft. 4ins. round his waist and 3ft. 1 ins. round his calf. He was teetotal and only ate one dish at a meal. He was said to be a very friendly individual and after he had been pensioned off as a gaoler he would sometimes rent a room in London and invite people to pay a shilling to come and talk to him. In 1809 he went to Stamford to the races and stayed at the Wagon and Horses Inn. After breakfast he was being shaved when he had a heart attack and died. A window had to be taken out and a wall demolished to get his body out of the inn. His coffin took 112 sq. ft. of elm: it was 6ft. 4ins. long, 4ft. 4ins. wide and 2ft. 4ins. deep. It was mounted on wheels and it took 20 men to lower it down a ramp into his grave in St. Martin's churchyard, Stamford, where it is still well cared for. His gravestone of Swithland slate states that it was erected by his many friends in Leicester. The Wagon and Horses is still there but is now a dwelling house.

We now go under the pedestrian underpass and come to the surface at the lower end of **FRIAR LANE** with the entrance to the Southgates Underpass on the left. The underpass goes beneath the site of the Roman Forum. It was in **SOUTHGATES** that John Johnson, architect of the City Rooms, built the **CONSANGUINITARIUM** in 1792 as alms houses for impoverished members of his family. Southgates takes its name from the proximity of the **SOUTH GATE** near the bottom of Friar Lane, one of the four gates into the medieval town. Its location is now marked by a Blue Plaque in the Southgate pedestrian underpass. Friar Lane ran along the southern boundary of the Greyfriars Friary site: it was called Frere Lane in 1391, Fryer Lane in 1741 and had been given its present name by 1815. The south wall of the Roman and medieval towns followed the line of Friar Lane; Millstone Lane which runs parallel, was the site of the town ditch running on the outside of the wall. It is thought that the Roman South Gate was located between Marble Street and Wycliffe Street. A stonemason's yard nearby was the possible origin of Marble Street's name and Wycliffe Street commemorates John Wycliffe, rector of Lutterworth, who first had the Gospels translated into English. The street name was spelt Wickcliffe until 1900.

Robert Herrick bought the Friary site at the time of the dissolution of the monasteries and built the Greyfriars Manor House with four acres of garden and lived there in the second half of the sixteenth century. His great grandson sold it again in 1711 and in that year New Street, (which we saw on our first arm-chair tour), was cut through the garden from Friar Lane to St. Martins. Thomas Pares, a banker, bought the Manor House in 1776 and added two wings to it: the house faced Friar Lane behind a large forecourt and its walled garden extended to St. Martins. In the north-east corner of the garden was an old house which Pares converted into bank premises, styled the Leicestershire Bank, in 1800. Retaining the bank building, he sold the Manor House to Beaumont Burnaby in 1824. Nothing remains of it today and the site was purchased by the Corporation in 1866.

Number 17 Friar Lane, on the left, often referred to as **DR. BENFIELD'S HOUSE**, is a well-proportioned eighteenth century building which is being preserved - note its central Venetian-style window on the first floor.

At the end of Friar Lane we turn into **BERRIDGE STREET** which takes its name from the Berridge family who owned land in this area. In 1874 Berridge Street and Grey Friars were cut through the former Manor House garden. We cross **HORSEFAIR STREET** and continue along **POCKLINGTON'S WALK**. This was once part of John Pocklington's garden. He was a cattle auctioneer and a Freeman of Leicester. He was dismissed from the Borough Corporation for insolvency in 1766 but recovered and became Mayor in 1788. The Mayoralty proved to be expensive and in 1789 he could only pay 11s. 3d. in the pound on a debt of £20 due to Trinity Hospital. He died a poor man - a pensioner of the Corporation.

In 1804 the cattle market was moved from the Market Place (then called the 'Saturday Market Place') to the area where the **TOWN HALL** and Town Hall Square now stand. This is the origin of Horsefair Street's name - it was called Horsefair Lane in 1805.

For many years the Corporation had suffered from overcrowding at the Town Hall (the present Guildhall) and the problem had been the subject of many debates. In 1871 it was decided to hold a competition for the best design for a Town Hall, to be built on the Manor House site in Friar Lane, but when the new cattle market was built in Aylestone Road in 1872 the Horsefair Street site became vacant and the earlier scheme was abandoned. It was decided to build the new Town Hall on the vacant old cattle market site and to hold a competition for the best design. The committee, whose task it was to choose the most suitable plan, found it impossible to make up their minds and they decided to hold a ballot. The members were told to vote for the design they liked the least and the one with the fewest votes would win the competition. The winner was F. J. Hames, a young architect practising in London. He submitted a design in Queen Anne style and that part of the Town Hall which faces Town Hall Square was built faithfully to his specifications in Suffolk brick and Ketton stone, and was finished in 1876 at a total cost of £53,000. The part of the Town Hall fronting Bowling Green Street was built in the same style and added in 1932.

The tower is 145 feet high and was without a clock for several years, causing it to be a source of music hall jokes. A tender of £907 by E. T. Loseby for making the clock was accepted. He was well known for his accurate chronometers used on Polar expeditions. Unfortunately he was taken ill when he had only half finished making the movement and obtained one from John Smith & Sons of Derby and installed it partly at his own expense - he was paid £450. Though he did not make the clock, the dials, which are seven feet in diameter, all bear his name. In later years, when the Quarter Sessions and Assizes were sitting, the judge would be housed at the Assembly Rooms (now the City Rooms) and the clock chimes would be turned off to ensure that he had a good night's sleep!

The Council met for the last time in the old Town Hall on 7th August 1876 and went in procession to the new Town Hall where the Mayor, Alderman William Barfoot, was presented with a silver key. A Council meeting was then held followed by a dinner at the Corn Exchange, a fireworks display and a Mayor's Ball in the Assembly Rooms.

To the right of the entrance are two cameos carved in stone. That on the left of the foundation stone represents night with a crescent moon, an owl which flies at night-time and sleep-inducing poppy heads, while the carving on the right illustrates day with a rising sun, a duck in early morning flight, sunflowers and mushrooms which presumably have grown during the night.

The **FOUNTAIN** was the gift of Alderman, later Sir, Israel Hart. He was High Bailiff at the time of its presentation in 1879 and was Mayor four times, being knighted after his fourth mayoralty. He never divulged the cost but it is said that this was around £2,000. He had shrewdly promised the fountain on condition that the Corporation bought the ground which is now **TOWN HALL SQUARE** and laid it out as a public pleasure garden, so we have him to thank for both. The square was known as the Horsefair Leys when it was being used as the cattle market and cost £1,200 to lay out. During World War II one of the lawns was cultivated as an allotment to show the public how to 'dig for victory'. The square was refurbished in 1989 providing more space for public gatherings and a brick mosaic of the city's arms was laid in front of the main entrance. The fountain was cast in iron in Paris and is painted bronze: it was designed by the architect of the Town Hall, F. J. Hames. There is another one exactly like it in every detail in

Oporto, Portugal, and one must assume that it was cast from the same moulds.

The **SOUTH AFRICAN WAR MEMORIAL** on the corner of **EVERY STREET** was unveiled in July 1909 by Field Marshal Lord Grenfell. Every Street, which is pedestrianized, runs along the bottom side of Town Hall Square and is so-called because there used to be a cab rank with a shelter at the Bishop Street end, offering cabs to every street in Leicester!

BISHOP STREET on the south side of Town Hall Square was named after Alderman William Bishop who was Mayor of Leicester in 1782. In 1805 he owned the land on which the street was laid out in 1809. He was the landlord of the Three Crowns Inn on the corner of Granby Street and Horsefair Street. Note that there is a caduceus above each entrance to the General Post Office. These are heralds' wands and hence staffs used by messengers: they represent the caducei of Hermes, the Greek god of commerce and peace, and were the distinctive marks of heralds and ambassadors. Next door, the former Liberal Club still has a bust of Gladstone in its entrance. The finely proportioned Methodist Church a little further up the street, built in 1815, is the oldest building in Bishop Street. The former Sunday School is next door on the left.

The Reference Library was founded in 1862 and the present building, which was paid for by Andrew Carnegie the American steel magnate and philanthropist, was built in 1905. From 1892, for twenty years, all racing and betting news was clipped out of newspapers placed in the public reading room ' to diminish the facilities for folly'!

A public bowling green was laid out at the expense of the town in 1736 in part of the Horsefair Leys and gave its name to **BOWLING GREEN STREET** which runs at the back of the Town Hall. The site was sold for building in 1807.

The former Sun Alliance Building, now occupied by the Trustee Savings Bank, which stands in **HORSEFAIR STREET** on the north side of Town Hall Square was designed by Joseph Goddard and built in 1891. Around 1980 the rear was completely rebuilt and the beautiful facade, incorporating a combination of Flemish and English styles, was preserved. The facade of the old Royal Hotel nearby was similarly saved when the rear was rebuilt at around the same time.

The cinquefoil, pierced and with ermine tails, featured in the city's arms dates back to the twelfth century and was part of the arms of Robert de Beaumont the first Earl of Leicester. The crest of Leicester's arms, a wyvern - a legless dragon - comes from the arms of Thomas, second Earl of Lancaster (and Earl of Leicester), son of Edmund Crouchback. Because he was executed for treason at Pontefract in 1320, its wings are flecked with blood.

Town Hall Square with the sun shining and the fountain playing, is a peaceful place to relax and recover from our second armchair tour.

Town Hall Square Fountain *(Leicester City Council)*

Notes on Chapter 2
[1] transubstantiation: the belief that the blessing of bread and wine at Mass converts them into the body and blood of Christ.

OUT AND ABOUT IN LEICESTER

CHAPTER THREE

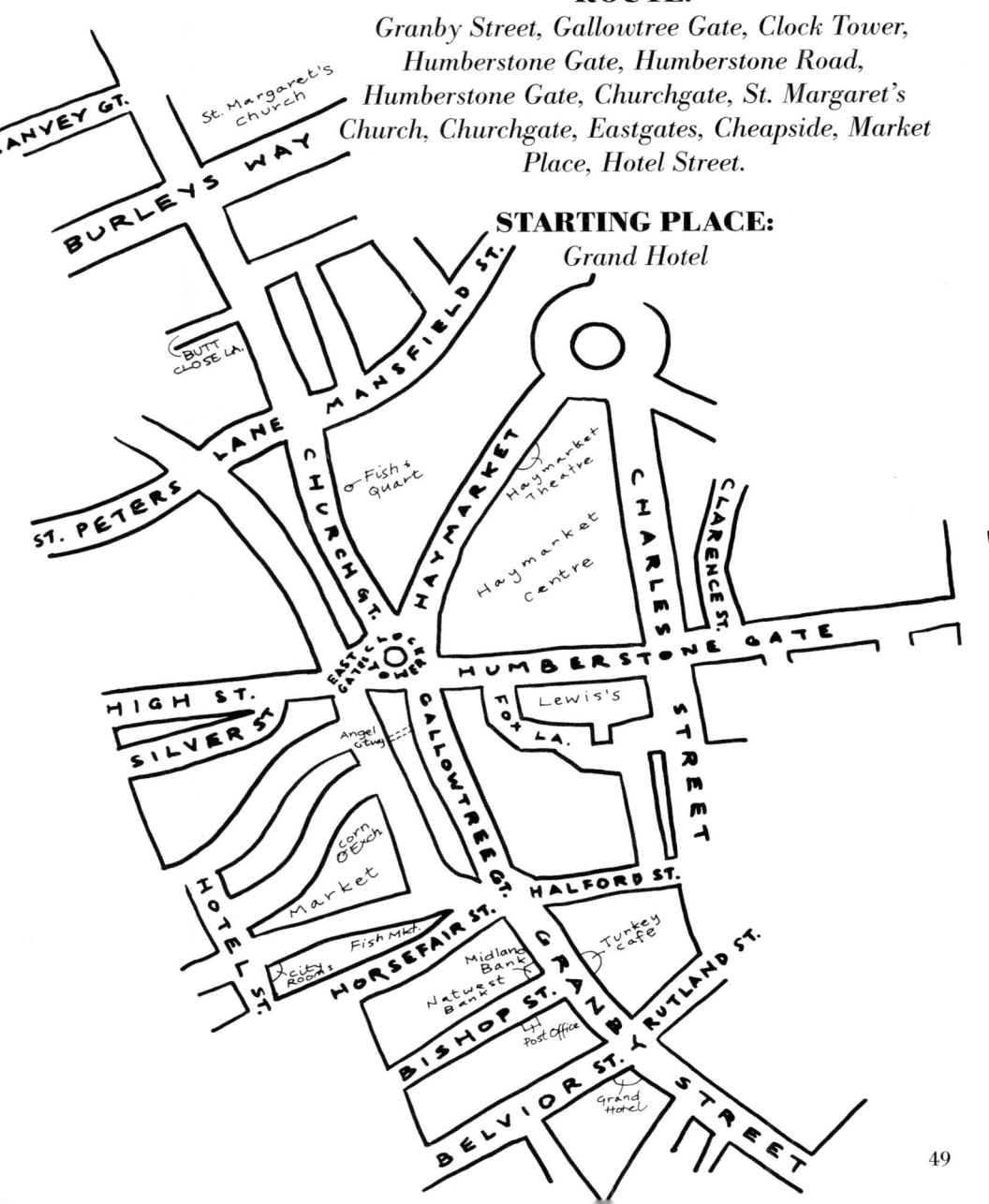

ROUTE:
Granby Street, Gallowtree Gate, Clock Tower, Humberstone Gate, Humberstone Road, Humberstone Gate, Churchgate, St. Margaret's Church, Churchgate, Eastgates, Cheapside, Market Place, Hotel Street.

STARTING PLACE:
Grand Hotel

49

Victoria Coffee House detail *(Leicester City Council)*

We begin our third armchair tour at the **GRAND HOTEL** standing on the corner of Granby Street and Belvoir Street. This used to be the site of the old Blue Lion, a Victorian public house which had a portico entrance with a sculptured recumbent lion lying on the portico roof in front of one of the bedroom windows. This pub was demolished along with much property higher up Granby Street to make way for the building of the Grand, one of Leicester's premier hotels. The main part of the hotel was built in 1898 in the English baroque style and designed by Cecil Ogden, but the corner, to the design of Amos Hall, surmounted by its superb decorative feature looking something like a Wren church, was built two years later. Embassy Hotels Ltd. restored the interior to its Victorian splendour a few years ago. It is now owned by Jarvis Hotels Ltd. **GRANBY STREET** takes its name from the Marquess of Granby (1721-1770), a professional soldier and son of the Duke of Rutland who owned land in this part of the town, and **BELVOIR STREET** from the Duke's principal residence, Belvoir Castle. This street was laid out in 1812 and before then the area was known as 'Cat Pye Gardens'.

RUTLAND STREET, across the road on the right, was laid out on land belonging to the Dukes of Rutland and was called 'Dogkennel Lane' at the beginning of the nineteenth century. Stable men from the Three Crowns and Three Cranes Inns used to wash their horses down in a horse pond near to where the **VICTORIA COFFEE HOUSE** stands today. This magnificent stone structure with its wonderful dome, minarets and turrets was designed by Edward Burgess and given this name because it was built in 1887 - the golden jubilee of Queen Victoria: the Duchess of Rutland opened it in the following year. It was one of twelve coffee houses owned by the Leicester Coffee and Cocoa House Company - a movement pioneered by Edward Shipley Ellis, Chairman of the Midland Railway Company. It was philanthropic in character, established on commercially profitable principles. It aimed to provide working men with an alternative to the public houses. In the Victorian era liquor was very cheap and many families suffered in consequence. Working men were encouraged to take their wrapped meals into the coffee houses and buy tea, coffee or other non-alcoholic drinks. They offered a breakfast service from 5 a.m. and could provide a basin of soup for 2d., a pint of tea or coffee for 1d., a bun or a cake for $^1/_2$d., or a full meal for 6d. There were rooms where games were played and where parents could take their children. The owners went out of business in 1922. Sir Herbert Marshall had his music shop on the ground floor of this building which was badly damaged in a disastrous fire in 1974 but has been restored to its original splendour.

The **GENERAL NEWS ROOM** built in a pseudo-classical style used to stand on the corner of Belvoir Street opposite the Grand Hotel. It housed the Permanent Library for many years and was demolished for road widening in 1898 to be replaced by the present impressive building, the first floor of which used to be one of the city's most exclusive restaurants and ballrooms. It was occupied by the Yorkshire Bank for some years and now by an estate agent with a jeweller on the ground floor. The General Post Office used to stand two doors away until it was replaced by the present GPO round the corner in **BISHOP STREET** in 1935. This street was named after Alderman William Bishop who was Mayor of Leicester in 1782: he owned the land on which the street was laid out in 1809 and was the landlord of the Three Crowns Inn.

Facing the bottom of Bishop Street is the **TURKEY CAFE**. This attractive building features turkey in two forms - the bird and the architect's idea of the Turkish style of architecture. It was designed and owned by Arthur Wakerley and built in 1900 specifically for his tenants, J. S. Winn & Co, who opened it as one of their many Leicester cafes. The front is faced with Carraraware tiles made by hand by William Neatby at the Lambeth pottery of Doulton & Company. The original shop-front was spoiled when the cafe was sold to another caterer but was restored to its original design in 1984 at a cost of £30,000 by the new occupants, Rayners the opticians, (now Dolland & Aitchison). By this time the original pottery had closed down and replacement tiles were made by Hathernware Ceramics of Loughborough.

There was an inn called 'The Jolly Miller' on the site of the Turkey Cafe in the eighteenth century and in 1610 a cock-pit stood nearby: it was a six-sided building with a domed roof. It is said to be highly probable that James I witnessed cock fights there on his several visits to Leicester.

Most will agree that the finest Victorian building in the city stands on the Bishop Street/Granby Street corner - the **MIDLAND BANK**. It was built as the Leicestershire Bank in Venetian Gothic style between 1872 and 1874 at a cost of £7,663 and designed by Joseph Goddard (1840-1900), the architect of many fine nineteenth century Leicester buildings. Notice the French pavilion style roofs, the red brick relieved by terracotta decorations and the stone carvings by Samuel Barfield. He carved much of the decorative stone-work on many Victorian buildings: look for the little monsters carved in Portland stone all over this bank. The Leicestershire Banking Company did not wish to be outdone by their rivals, the National & Provincial Bank, who had built new premises almost next door, so they had their headquarters designed on the grand scale. The banking hall is just as impressive as the exterior. It is now the Midland Bank's principal Leicester branch.

The **NATIONAL WESTMINSTER BANK** only a door or two away was built in Italianate style in 1869 to the design of William Millican. It stands on the site of the **THREE CROWNS INN**, Leicester's most famous coaching inn, built in 1726 and named to commemorate the recent union of the crown of Hanover with those of England and Scotland in the person of George I. It was here that the four medieval town gates were sold by auction on 21st March 1774 for building materials and in that year the first

Leicester coach service began. When the High Cross was demolished in 1773 three of its pillars were brought to the Three Crowns - two were used to make a portico and one to prop up the ceiling of the principal room. The last stage coach left here in 1866 and four years later the inn itself was closed to make way for the bank.

We now enter **GALLOWTREE GATE** - its name is a grim reminder of the public executions of years ago. It used to run from where the Clock Tower now stands to Victoria Park Road and the gallows were at the top of the present London Road at the end of the Evington Footway, nearly opposite the Victoria Park Gates. The Market Place side of Gallowtree Gate follows the line of the medieval east wall which ran from Sanvey Gate to Horsefair Street and the present street was the ditch on the outside of the wall. These ditches in time became filled in, making slopes from the walls. The slopes were divided into small plots, mainly used as gardens and orchards. Some parts of the slopes had houses and barns on them. The earliest post-Roman **TOWN WALLS**, following the lines of the Roman walls, were said to have been built by Ethelfleda, Queen of Mercia, daughter of Alfred the Great, King of Wessex, after she had re-taken Leicester from the Danes in 918. They were demolished during the insurrection of Henry 'the young king' against his father, Henry II, in which he was joined by Robert 'Blanchmains', the third Earl of Leicester: they were subsequently re-built. The walls were broad and were a burden on the citizens who had to keep them in repair at the expense of the community. In the later Middle Ages they became less important for defensive purposes and served as a means of channelling traders and others through the gates where tolls known as 'murage' could be levied to pay for wall repairs. In the sixteenth century an additional gate called the 'Goltre Gate', a corruption of Gallowtree Gate, was opened into the Market Place at the south-east corner of the town walls. Market Approach, made in the late nineteenth century, leading from the Horsefair Street/Gallowtree Gate corner into the Market Place, occupies this site. The passages such as Victoria Parade, leading from Gallowtree Gate to the market, originated as gaps cut in the east wall.

One of the first buildings we see on the left on Gallowtree Gate began life as the **PELICAN INN** built in 1882. It is an attractive building - notice the pargetting, the decorative plaster work, above the windows of the second floor. It used to have a balcony too above this level but this disappeared some years ago. Nearly next door the **ROBIN HOOD** public house stood with another attractive building adjoining. This was the Criterion Restaurant for ten years and for fifty years a bank, finally becoming a cake shop and an employment agency. Both were demolished in 1989 to make way for a clothing store. Many changes have been made in this street - not always for the better. Older citizens will remember Adderlys which ruled Gallowtree Gate for 90 years, later becoming Marshall & Snelgroves. Their beautiful building was pulled down and replaced by a modern concrete fronted structure.

Boots the Chemists store, on the right hand side of the street, stands on the site of the **THREE CRANES INN**. Passing Victoria Parade on the left we come to **THE ANGEL GATEWAY** leading to **MORLEY ARCADE** named for Morleys' two shops at the Cheapside end, well known for their haberdashery, fabrics and curtains. Richard Morley pioneered half-day closing for shops. If we walk half-way through the Arcade and look high up to the right we can see a part of a timber framed building. This is a portion of the old **ANGEL INN**. Mary Queen of Scots stayed here on 22nd and 23rd September 1586 on her way to Fotheringhay for trial and execution.

Notice the two stone faces carved by Crosland McClure to the left and right of the entrance to the former **BARCLAY'S BANK** (now a men's outfitters), a few doors farther along from Boots. One face has its eyes open and the other closed, representing 'sleeping' and 'waking'. Did they signify that the bank would care for one's money at all times?

Joseph Goddard was the designer of **THOMAS COOK'S FORMER OFFICES** built in 1894 on the left side of Gallowtree Gate near the Clock Tower. The interesting features of this building are the four terracotta plaques at the upper first floor level, all alluding to landmarks in the career of this pioneer of world travel. He was born at Melbourne in Derbyshire in 1808 and had a very poor start in life when his father died four years later. At the age of ten he worked as an under-gardener for a penny a day. When his master had bouts of drunkenness young Thomas had to hawk his produce round the streets of Melbourne on a barrow. He worked as a wood-turner, then a printer and started his own printing business which was not a success.

He was living at Market Harborough and, as a keen advocate of temperance, he one day walked the fourteen miles to Leicester to attend a Temperance Society meeting at the old Amphitheatre in Humberstone Gate. As he walked he had an inspiration: a temperance rally was to be held at Southfields Park at Loughborough, why not hire a train and take a party to it from Leicester? A train had been hired only once before in Leicester when

'Thomas Cook' plaques *(Leicester City Council)*

a party from the Nottingham Mechanics Institute came to see an exhibition organised by Leicester's Institute, so to run an excursion would give the rally good publicity. He sold tickets at one shilling return which included entertainment by a brass band on the journey and tea and buns on arrival at the park. Five hundred and seventy people bought tickets and the first plaque shows the year 1841 and a typical Victorian train with no seats or roofs to the carriages, drawn by an engine a little like Stephenson's Rocket. The date was 5th July and there were eight third class carriages and the guard rode in the single first class carriage. The band squeezed in with the passengers and 3,000 people gathered to watch them depart in a shower of smoke and sparks. The success of this first trip was ultimately to lead to Thomas Cook establishing his travel business when the spread of rail travel in Britain and on the Continent was to lead to the dawn of new horizons.

The second plaque is dated 1851 - the year of the Great Exhibition in Hyde Park in London. Notice the Crystal Palace on the left, (it was moved to Sydenham when the exhibition was over and was eventually burned down), and a rather more modern train. Cook's travel firm organised excursions to the exhibition from towns and cities all over the country, carrying a total of 165,000 passengers. His travel company grew when he promoted excursions to English spas and seaside resorts, and the Paris exhibition of 1855 introduced him to organising holidays all over the Continent.

The opening of the Suez Canal in 1869 brought about the opening up of Egypt and the Middle East for tourists, and by the 1880s Thomas Cook & Son had developed a monopoly of Nile passenger traffic with their own fleet of Nile steamers which they had built in Scotland, shipped out in pieces and assembled at Alexandria. The third terracotta panel bears the date 1884: in this year the company was commissioned by the British government to transport an expeditionary force of 18,000 men and 100,000 tons of supplies up the Nile from Alexandria to relieve General Gordon who was being besieged at Khartoum by the Mahdi. Fifty Nile steamers and 650 sailing boats were used and the cost was £600,000. Unfortunately the expedition arrived too late - General Gordon had been murdered. The plaque shows the pyramids, a Nile steamer and sailing boats.

The fourth panel bears the date 1891 - the Golden Jubilee of Thomas Cook and Son. The Forth railway bridge featured on the panel had been opened in the previous year. By this time Thomas Cook was blind and the business was being run by his son, John Mason Cook. Thomas died a year later.

What became the first traffic island to be constructed in Great Britain, the **CLOCK TOWER**, or to give it its official title, the Haymarket Memorial Clock Tower, stands right in front of us. Hay, straw and other agricultural produce were sold on this spot from the twelfth century. There must have been a mound here for in the Borough records of 1260 the area, which was outside the east wall of the town, was known as 'Berehill' ('bere' is a Saxon word meaning agricultural produce in general and barley in particular). A cross stood on the mound which was referred to as the 'Berehill Cross' in 1484, and beneath it was a set of stocks, a pillory and a cage for the punishment of delinquents. The East Gate was nearby, roughly opposite where New Bond Street was, but the farm carts could not pass through it, or any of the other town gates, which were too low and too narrow. By the early sixteenth century Leicester speech had corrupted 'Berehill' to 'Barrel' and the 'Barrel Cross' which stood here was demolished in 1575.

The mound later became known as 'The Roundle', 'The Round Hill' and by 1700 as 'Coal Hill'. Coal, brought in panniers on

The Clock Tower area early this century *(Leicester City Council)*

the backs of pack-horses and donkeys from the Leicestershire pits was sold here. In 1750 John Bass, who owned part of the site, built the **ASSEMBLY ROOMS**. They projected from East Gates into the present Clock Tower area. At the east end of the building were four columns facing Humberstone Gate which supported the stage of the Coal Hill Theatre on the upper floor. Beneath the colonnade there was a weighing machine used in the sale of coal and wood for fuel until the Leicester Canal, opened in 1794, and later the railways, made other arrangements more convenient.

By the middle of the nineteenth century the Assembly Rooms were becoming dilapidated; the streets surrounding them were very narrow and the passage of traffic was a problem. A committee was formed in 1862 which bought the building and demolished it. The vacant space, by this time known as the Haymarket, was paved and it appeared that the cause of congestion had been solved but the sale of farm produce continued as before and spread over the greater space made available and the obstruction was as bad as ever. In an effort to overcome the difficulty the sale of hay and straw was moved to the upper end of Humberstone Gate in 1867. Now horse-drawn traffic converging from six streets into the Haymarket caused chaos and to sort out the tangle the Improvement Committee was re-convened and decided to build the Haymarket Memorial Clock Tower, to form a traffic island and pedestrian refuge which in turn would create a gyratory traffic flow.

The Clock Tower was to be a memorial to four benefactors of Leicester. The competition which was held to secure the best design was won by Joseph Goddard who was aged only 28. The total cost was £949 - between £800 and £900 was raised by public subscription and the Borough Corporation paid the balance. Samuel Barfield was awarded the stone masonry contract. At the foundation stone laying nothing was placed under the stone so, when the top stone was laid, a bottle containing coins, newspapers and details of members of the Corporation was placed beneath it. Ketton Stone was used for the most part: the statues, which cost £37.10s. each, are of Portland stone, and Peterhead granite and polished serpentine were used for the shafts at the angles of the tower. The clock was operated by weights but it has since been electrified. The work was completed in 1868.

The four benefactors were Simon de Montfort, Earl of Leicester, who remitted certain taxes; William Wyggeston, founder of Wyggeston's Hospital and whose money was used after his death to found the Free Grammar School; Alderman Gabriel Newton who founded Alderman Newton's School; and Sir Thomas White, founder of the charity bearing his name which lent money without interest to enable young men to start in business.

Beneath the Clock Tower there is a large inspection chamber for a section of the city's sewerage system. It is lined with glazed brick and there is room for about thirty people to stand inside it. It was opened to public view for two days in 1972 when some of the space round about was laid out as a pedestrian area with seats and trees.

In 1777 Thomas Pettifor of the nearby Stag and Pheasant Inn introduced a hackney coach stand at Coal Hill: he charged one shilling for up to four people to any place in Leicester.

Now we will turn into **HUMBERSTONE GATE**, looking first at the right hand side and then returning to the Clock Tower down the left side. Ollerenshaw's fish and chip restaurant, which had a great reputation, used to stand on the site of the store on the corner of Fox Lane.

LEWIS'S store, built in 1935, which has enjoyed considerable popularity over the years, was sold in 1991 for £38m for redevelopment. It was closed down early in 1994 and is due to be demolished and replaced by shops. The Tower, which has been a landmark for over half a century, is to be retained. In 1938 a large air-raid siren with two revolving horns was installed on the top of the tower: its spine-chilling warning could be heard over a wide area of the City. Hamshaw's Garage was next to Lewis's: when it was moved to new premises in Welford Road the old garage was pulled down to enable Lewis's to be extended.

With an eye on the fast-moving traffic we cross what used to be referred to as 'Leicester's Million Pound Street' - **CHARLES STREET**. The original street bearing this name was narrow and lined with terraced houses and ran between Humberstone Gate and Northampton Square. It was named after Charles II following the Restoration in 1660. The modern dual carriageway was opened in 1932. It was designed to take traffic away from the Clock Tower area and at the time it was thought that it would become Leicester's principal shopping street, but is now being partially pedestrianized.

The first old building we come to on the far side of Charles Street is the **SECULAR HALL,** the only surviving purpose built secular hall outside London. It existed to debate free thought and every burning issue of the day. The hall was designed by Larner Sugden and opened in 1881. Secularism was described as 'less negative than atheism' and the Gimson family were among the leading figures in the local movement. The hall was built when George Jacob Holyoake (1817-1906), a leading national Secularist was denied the use of the public room at the Three Crowns Inn for a lecture. Five busts in terracotta by Vago, form a unique feature on the façade: they represent Socrates, Voltaire, Robert Owen, Thomas Paine and Jesus Christ. The Secular Hall is a Grade II Listed Building and in 1990 an appeal was made for £100,000 to pay for its restoration.

The **VESTRY HALL** used to stand near the end of Humberstone Gate. The members of St. Margaret's Select Vestry used to meet here every month to administer the several charities which provided support for impoverished persons living within the bounds of the old St. Margaret's parish, which extended nearly to the top of London Road. Part of the hall was used as a Juvenile Court. It was demolished in the early 1980s and replaced by a block of flats.

Facing us on the corner of Rutland Street and Humberstone Road is the site of the former headquarters of Freeman, Hardy & Willis, the largest company of footwear distributors in Britain before World War II. Their building was gutted by bombing and fire in an air-raid carried out by over 100 German bombers on the night of November 19-20 1940. After the war the company became a part of the British Shoe Corporation which rebuilt the warehouse on the same site but later replaced it by huge premises in Sunningdale Road. The Rutland Street building had a tower block added on the corner and was converted into the Magnum Hotel. In turn this has become the Centre Hotel, the Leicester International Hotel, the Ladbroke Hotel, the Penguin Hotel and is now the **PARK INTERNATIONAL HOTEL**.

Near the end of Humberstone Gate, in the centre of the roadway, is the Victorian **WEIGHBRIDGE**, built in 1867 following the transfer of the sale of hay and straw to this site in 1862. It incorporated a toll-collector's house. It was cleaned externally in the later 1980s and is now used as a taxi office. The **MAY** and **MICHAELMAS FAIRS** were held in Humberstone Gate - in 1895 the date of the latter was altered from 10th October to the second Thursday in October by which time they had become purely pleasure fairs. The last one was held in October 1904 after which they were transferred to Ross Walk, and the Corporation voted £20,000 to meet claims for compensation. An area of the roadway near the weighbridge was enclosed and re-paved in 1993 and will be available for open air functions.

In the distance, down Humberstone Road, the attractive Regency red brick building known as **SPA PLACE** can be seen on the left. Following the discovery of a chalybeate spring here in 1789 an attempt was made to run a spa. It was still advertised in 1793 but was closed down early in the nineteenth century. On the wall of the present building, which has been recently restored, is an interesting plaque commemorating Queen Victoria's Diamond Jubilee. On the same side of the road, on the Wharf Street corner, is the high rise **CARDINAL TELEPHONE EXCHANGE** which handles international calls.

We now cross Humberstone Gate and make our way back towards the Clock Tower. Zoots, a night club, used to be the **PALAIS DE DANSE**. It was built by the Batten family between 1925 and 1928 on the site of their coal and hay merchants business at 66 Humberstone Gate. With its fountain in the middle of the dance floor, it is remembered with nostalgia by many older people. The Age Concern building, known as **CLARENCE HOUSE**, was built as the Wyggeston Girls' School and designed by Edward Burgess. It accommodated 300 girls and in 1928 was occupied by the City of Leicester Boys School when the girls moved to their new premises on Regent Road. When the boys' school was moved to Downing Drive, Evington, the building was used as an annexe to Charles Keene College, finally being acquired by Age Concern in the early 1980s and given its present name. The house to the left of the entrance was built as a home for the headmistress.

CLARENCE STREET, named after the Duke of Clarence who later became King William IV, is the narrow street between Clarence House and number 44 Humberstone Gate - Green's Television and Video store. This building dates from 1869 when it was built as John Meadows' Midland Distillery. It contained not only a distillery and warehouse but had a finely panelled smoking room over the front entrance where customers could meet and do business in a congenial atmosphere.

We cross Charles Street again and come to the **HAYMARKET CENTRE** which was built in the early 1970s and takes up the whole of this side of this half of Humberstone Gate. To build it a number of old-established businesses and public houses had to be closed and the tram sheds, with the old stables housing the horses which pulled the early trams, were demolished. The loss of the Bell Hotel, an old coaching inn, is particularly regretted by older citizens. It was much used as a venue for conferences, parties and receptions and its lovely ballroom was very popular.

Back at the Clock Tower, which is usually considered to be the centre of the city - commercially if not geographically - we who have lived in Leicester for many years will recall how the traffic at this busy spot used to be controlled by two policemen on point-duty: it eventually reached such a high volume that steps had to be taken to deal with the problem with the result that virtually all private vehicles have now been banished from the city's centre. Going back beyond the memories of most citizens, the tramlines which were laid round the Clock Tower in 1903 formed the most complicated system of tramway junctions in Britain.

Looking down Belgrave Gate we see where the **PALACE THEATRE** once stood, opposite its replacement, the **HAYMARKET THEATRE**; the first demolished in the late 1960s and the latter built around 1973. The interior of the Palace was beautifully decorated in the oriental style but it could not compete with television and had to go, along with the old Opera House in Silver Street and, some years before, the Theatre Royal in Horsefair Street - losses mourned by many theatre goers.

The **EASTGATES COFFEE HOUSE**, on the corner of East Gates and Church Gate, was another of the twelve owned by the Leicester Coffee and Cocoa House Company. It was built in what was described as 'Nuremburg Gothic' style in 1885 and designed by Edward Burgess. The walls of the ground floor consisted of a series of arches: these have long since gone but the upper floors remain just as they were built. The premises on the opposite corner were rebuilt a few years ago but many will remember the Bovril advertising sign which decorated the previous structure, its multitude of coloured lights forming constantly changing patterns.

CHURCH GATE was known as 'Kyrkegate' in 1478 but had been given its present name by the beginning of the seventeenth century. It is literally the road ('gata') to the church (St. Margaret's). The horse-drawn trams which ran along Church Gate was called 'the Church Gate Express' because only one horse was needed as the gradient was slight!

We come to **MANSFIELD STREET** on the right, named after John Mansfield, a banker, who was Mayor of Leicester in 1815: its earlier name was Ploughman Lane. In the nineteenth century **ST. PETER'S LANE** opposite, was called Women's Lane. It led to the ancient church of St. Peter, demolished in the second half of the sixteenth century.

Branigan's night club on the right, formerly Gatsby's, used to be the **FISH AND QUART** public house which was one of the buildings designed in 1832 by Henry Goddard, father of the architect of the Clock Tower. From time to time circuses would come to Leicester and put on performance at the Palace Theatre. Some animals had to be caged but the more docile ones were brought out of the theatre's rear entrance in Mansfield Street and stabled at the back of the Fish and Quart. The doorway to the left of the building was made especially high so that the elephants could go through!

We go through the pedestrian underpass under **BURLEY'S WAY** - part of the inner ring road - and surface outside the Prebendal **CHURCH OF ST. MARGARET,** which had a special relationship with the Bishops of Lincoln. This is the third church to stand on this site; the first which was built in the Saxon era was the Cathedral when the Leicester Diocese was first established in 679 AD. When the Danes invaded and the Leicester Bishopric was removed to Dorchester in the 870s, jurisdiction over St. Margaret's was transferred to Lincoln. The church was always outside the town walls. There was a major rebuilding programme towards the end of the thirteenth century, except for the massive tower and clerestory which were built in 1444 and paid for by a 'smoke farthing' - a local hearth tax levied by the Bishop of Lincoln. The foundations of an earlier Norman church were uncovered in the 1940s and may be seen beneath a glass panel in the floor. Notice the grooves, worn by archers sharpening their arrow points in the stonework, surrounding the south doorway.

The west end of the church faces **SANVEY GATE** which in 1322 was called the 'Skeyth' - the Danish word for racecourse. The old town racecourse was on the meadows nearby (now known as St. Margaret's Pasture), but it was moved to a site near the present Royal Infirmary because the ground was too boggy. By 1392 the street was referred to as 'Sanvey Gate'. Maps showed it as 'Sinvis Gate' in 1610 and 'Sandy Gate' in 1805. It had been given its present spelling by 1815.

'Sanvey' is thought to be a corruption of 'Sancta Via', its ancient name, meaning 'The Holy Way'. The road was given its name because of a solemn procession which passed through it on Whit-Monday beginning at St. Mary de Castro Church and ending at St. Margaret's. It was led by minstrels playing harps and other instruments. Then came an image of the Virgin, which normally had a place of honour in St. Mary's Church, carried beneath a canopy borne by four men. Following on came twelve men each

St.. Margaret's Church *(Leicester City Council)*

representing one of the twelve apostles, with the names of the apostles, written on parchment, fixed to their bonnets. Behind them came persons bearing banners and the virgins of the parish. On the way they were joined by another procession from St. Martin's Church, led by an image of their patron saint. A service was held and after the ceremony the participants returned to St. Mary's where they were regaled at the expense of the parish - in 1513 a calf was provided at a cost of 2s. 4d.! The custom was abolished in 1559, following the Reformation.

As we return up Church Gate we pass **BUTT CLOSE LANE,** on the right hand side, whose name provides an interesting reminder of the past. Queen Elizabeth I gave $1^{1}/_{2}$ acres of land in Church Gate to the Freeman of Leicester for the practice of archery - hence the name Butt Close. It was held by the Borough Corporation from the Duchy of Lancaster by the presentation annually of a broad arrow - the Chamberlains' accounts show 4d. having been paid for it. The exercise of the longbow was enforced by Act of Parliament. All male persons over the age of seven years were obliged to practise in the butts at stated times, each with his own bow of length equal to his own height, and with at least two arrows: as already mentioned the arrow points were sharpened on the stonework of St. Margaret's Church nearby. The Queen was aware of the threat of Spanish invasion and a force of practised archers was a prudent safeguard. Archery had been practised as long ago as the Hundred Years War, but when gunpowder came into use it declined. By the beginning of the nineteenth century the Butt Close was being used for a wood yard and orchards.

A little higher up Church Gate, on the same side as Butt Close Lane, there is a large wooden warehouse, a listed building, build in 1820. It was originally owned by Thomas Brown, a timber merchant: he probably built it to store timber and as a workshop. For many years Worthington's, who owned a chain of grocery shops all over Leicester, used it as a grocery warehouse. They went out of business when supermarkets took over.

We continue up Church Gate and cross East Gates. If we had been here before the trams were replaced by buses, and had looked towards the junction of Silver Street and High Street, on a triangular island we should have seen the barriers which served to control the queues of passengers waiting for trams serving three or four routes. On Saturday nights, at the point of the triangle, the roast potato man would be plying his trade, cooking his potatoes in an oven which looked something like Stephenson's Rocket.

The street name **CHEAPSIDE** is of Saxon origin: 'Cheap' meaning 'a market', is from 'ceapan' meaning 'to buy'. The street's old English name was 'Chepe'. 'Cheapside' first appeared on maps at the beginning of the nineteenth century. The name is appropriate, for the road leads to the Market Place where a market has been held for hundreds of years. The most eye-catching feature in Cheapside is the single pillar of the **HIGH CROSS** -

the only remaining one of the original eight. When this pillar was removed from its site on the High Street/Highcross Street corner in 1836, it was purchased by James Rawson, whose father and uncle had both been Mayors of Leicester. He re-erected it in front of the Crescent in King Street, which he owned. In 1919 Arthur Wakerley, an architect, bought the Crescent and used one of the houses as an office. In 1923 he moved the pillar to the garden of a house he had built for his daughter in Gwendolen Road. In 1954 it was again removed and set up in the garden of the Newarke Houses Museum. In 1977, to celebrate its sixtieth anniversary, the Leicester Rotary Club paid for the pillar to be set up on its present site and for the area to be laid out as a pedestrian area.

The **CONDUIT**, built in 1612, used to stand near the present site of the High Cross pillar. It was a leaden cistern enclosed in an octagonal brick structure with a pointed slated roof. Water was brought from a spring in St. Margaret's Field which was near the old Hillcrest Hospital, (the former Workhouse), in lead pipes down Conduit Street, (this is the origin of the street's name), to the Market Place where it was stored in the cistern. It was said that the water was very good for making tea! On several occasions of great public rejoicing, for example on the accession of George IV, the Conduit was made to run with ale or wine for the benefit of the lower classes.

In 1841 the octagonal building was taken down and rebuilt at Wigston where it decayed and was eventually demolished to make way for a school. In its place a column surmounted by a lamp was put up. In 1852 this was replaced by a bronze statue of the fifth Duke of Rutland which had a water tap in its pedestal. When the Leicester Waterworks were established in 1853 the water supply was cut off. The Duke's statue, sculpted by Edward Davis, which commemorated his fifty years as Lord Lieutenant of the County, was moved to the centre of the Market Place in 1872. It was gilded at this time but no trace of gold can be found today. It was moved again to a site near West Bridge in 1931 and, when the Market Place was re-organised in 1971, returned to its present position - roughly where it had been between 1872 and 1931 but facing south-east instead of north-east.

Much of the old **ANGEL INN** still stands at the back of what is now the Victoria Wine Shop. When this was Blackman's tobacco store more of the old structure was preserved but has now been destroyed.

As we go into the **MARKET PLACE** notice the bollards at the entrance to Victoria Parade: they all bear the date 1848. This was a year of revolution in Europe, and in anticipation that similar trouble might spread to England, the bollards were put in place to slow down any rioting mobs.

The authority to hold markets came not by a charter from the King, but from the Earl: the oldest documentary record is dated 1298. This is why Leicester market used to be called the 'Earl's Market' though its most common name was the 'Saturday Market'. There was no shelter for the vendors until a building was put up on the site of the present **CORN EXCHANGE** in the mid-fifteenth century to accommodate the butchers and clothing dealers. The butchers had to pay a rent of $1^{1}/_{2}$d. per stall to the Duchy of Lancaster. There have been at least five buildings on the Corn Exchange site. The ground floor of the present Corn Exchange was built in 1850, replacing the 'New Gainsborough' - officially called 'The Exchange' - built in 1748, which in turn had replaced the 'Gainsborough' put up in 1509. The Gainsborough was used partly as a prison and law courts, and partly as shops: it had a dungeon in its cellar. It was damaged by soldiers in the Siege of Leicester during the Civil War in 1645. Six years after the single storey building had been erected in 1850 it was decided to put another storey on top of it and, to avoid spoiling the new building by putting in an internal staircase, the architect put the stairs outside - this accounts for the arched double staircase which is reminiscent of Venice. In the centre of the front of the arch is a little stone figure which looks distinctly medieval; perhaps it was salvaged from one of the earlier buildings. It is clearly something to do with brewing for he carried a sheaf of barley (until his arm was broken off a year or two ago) and has barley growing near his feet which stand upon a tun or barrel. Farmers sold their grain, probably by showing samples, on the upper floor of the Corn Exchange which was also used for functions, and cheese was sold on the ground floor.

The weather vane on the Corn Exchange clock tower is a **WYVERN**. This mythical beast, which is normally depicted with wings and two legs (a dragon has four), is legless. It is the crest of the city's arms and originated as the crest of Thomas, Earl of Lancaster. He succeeded his father, Edmund Crouchback, the second surviving son of Henry III, as Earl. Earl Thomas plotted with a group of disaffected barons against the King and was beheaded without trial for treason outside Pontefract in 1323, and all his possessions were seized by the Crown. For this reason Leicester's wyvern crest is flecked with blood, representing bleeding wounds.

Running along the market side of the east wall of the medieval town walls was a broad pavement known as the **CORN WALL**. Here farmers would sell their corn and dealers would sell horses. The ringing of a bell ten times signalled the opening of trading and it was closed in the same way. When there was no market everything had to be cleared away - an offender was liable to be fined 12d. A man was paid 13s. 4d. per year to clear up the Market Place after the Saturday market - he had to finish the job by Tuesday.

Besides being a regular Saturday retail market and being used by farmers to sell their grain and horses, the Market Place was used as a cattle market from 1341 to 1597, when it was moved to Cank Street and Loseby Lane. It was moved back again for a short time between 1793 and 1804 and was then transferred to the Horsefair Leys, (the present Town Hall Square). There was a pinfold on the site of the former **FISH MARKET** in the sixteenth century: stray cattle and sheep were put into it until they were claimed by their owners who had to pay a small fee to recover them. The Fish Market was built in 1877 and has been preserved and converted into shops.

The medieval inns in or near the Market Place relied on the farmers who patronised them both for refreshment and for stabling their horses. There was a well known one called the Old Green Dragon near the Corn Wall. Nearby, from the reign of Elizabeth I to early in the nineteenth century, there was a huge elm known as the Pigeon Tree - country folk bred pigeons for food and sold them beneath this tree. Also under the tree was a set of stocks, a pillory and a gibbet.

The Market Place was used for public meetings of all kinds and many famous politicians have addressed huge throngs here, but since the market stalls were permanently fixed in 1971 this has not been possible. In that year the Market Place was roofed with fibre-glass 'egg-crate' sections which were the cause of endless trouble - a familiar sight was the dozens of buckets which caught rainwater from the many leaks. In 1991 a new roof was installed. The new **MARKET CENTRE** was built around 1978, providing a considerable extension under cover to the market accommodation

City Rooms *(Leicester City Council)*

replacing the old Fish Market and providing new hygienic facilities for the sale of meat. Many market traders sell goods from Leicester's textile and shoe manufacturing factories and the market generally has the reputation of being one of the finest, if not the finest in the country.

Passing the Market Centre on the right we reach the **CITY ROOMS**, built around 1792, on the corner facing the junction of Hotel Street and Friar Lane. **HOTEL STREET** is something of an oddity for it has never had an hotel in it, but what we now call the City Rooms was intended to be an hotel to cater for visitors to the Races. This Palladian style building, decorated by figures of the Comic and Lyric Muses by Vago, standing on the site of an eighteenth century cock-pit, was designed by John Johnson, Leicester's first professional architect, (craftsmen used to call themselves architects if their work involved an element of design). It was to be called an hotel to indicate its superiority over the many common inns. Unfortunately financial problems arose before the building was finished and the original project had to be abandoned. The unfinished building was sold to a group of gentlemen who made the ground floor into a coffee house and used the upper floor for banquets, wedding receptions, balls and similar functions. In 1817 they too got into difficulty and sold the premises to the Quarter Sessions of the Leicestershire Magistrates, as a lodging for the judge when he was presiding over the Assizes and Quarter Sessions, and as a repository for the county records.

From the time it was formed in 1889, the Leicestershire County Council met quarterly in what became known as the **COUNTY ROOMS**. Their last meeting there was in 1967 - two years before they moved to the new County Hall at Glenfield. In 1986 the County Rooms were exchanged by the County Council for the Lord Mayor's Rooms at the New Walk Museum, the City Council paying an additional £100,000. They were then renamed the City Rooms.

Inside the entrance hall of the City Rooms is a bronze statue of **QUEEN ÆTHELFLOEDA.** The original statue formed part of a drinking fountain which stood in Victoria Park, near the Granville Road entrance. It was a memorial to Edith Gittins, artist and social reformer, (1845-1910). Æthelfloeda was the Queen of Mercia and the daughter of King Alfred the Great. She was successful in driving the Danes out of this part of Mercia in 918 A.D. The statue was stolen in 1978 and, when Dolphin Square was created in the Market Place at the rear of the former Sun Alliance Building, the drinking fountain with a replacement statue was installed in the centre. It was unveiled in 1980 and the statue was stolen ten days later. After it had been stolen yet again, but recovered, the fountain was removed and replaced by a tree surrounded by seating. In 1990 the statue was installed in the City Rooms where it should be safe from further vandalism.

Next door to the City Rooms on the Market Place side, a small theatre was built: it was also designed by John Johnson. It was very plain, built of brick.

Thetare Royal, Horsefair Street *(Leicester City Council)*

It was opened in March 1800 but was demolished in 1836. The old Theatre Royal was later built on the same site but it fronted Horsefair Street.

This the end of our third armchair tour - perhaps an appropriate place to relax and reflect on what we have seen or learned about.

OUT AND ABOUT IN LEICESTER

CHAPTER FOUR

ROUTE:
Bowling Green Street, Belvoir Street, Welford Place, King Street, New Walk, University Road, Regent Road, King Street, Welford Place, Pocklington's Walk

STARTING PLACE:
Horsefair Street/ Bowling Green Street corner

Former Water Department Office, Bowling Green Street *(Leicester City Council)*

For our fourth arm-chair tour we meet on the corner of Horsefair Street and Bowling Green Street. One of the principal offices of the Alliance & Leicester Building Society stands on the other side of Horsefair Street on the site of the old **THEATRE ROYAL**. This theatre, called by this name officially from 1851 though it was built in 1836, was fronted by four massive square pillars. With seats for 1,300 it was uneconomically small and its acoustics were the subject of severe criticism when it was new. It suffered from the competition of the Amphitheatre in Humberstone Gate which seated 3,000 but was a failure and was demolished in 1848, only eight years after it was built. The Opera House in Silver Street and later the Palace in Belgrave Gate brought further competition: the town could not support three theatres and all had disappeared by 1960 - it used to be said that there were three disastrous weeks in the theatre, the week before Christmas, Holy Week, and a week in Leicester! Though in later years the theatre generally did not flourish in Leicester, some famous actors, including Henry Irving appeared at the Theatre Royal.

That part of the **TOWN HALL** which faces Bowling Green Street was built in 1924 as an extension in exact conformity with F. J. Hames' original design. The building had a narrow escape during World War II when a high-explosive bomb fell through the roof and failed to go off. The Town Hall was soon found to be too small and was supplemented by large new Municipal Offices in Charles Street, which in turn were vacated with the move to the **NEW WALK CENTRE**. This move left the Town Hall with some vacant accommodation and there is a body of opinion which advocates its use as a Registry Office.

Passing Bishop Street on the left we come to the former **WATER DEPARTMENT OFFICE**, designed by Shenton & Baker in what has been described as 'municipal Gothic' - the first secular building in Leicester to be built in this style. Notice how the different periods of Gothic are featured: the ground floor in perpendicular style; the first floor in early English style and the section on the right, with its projecting door and oriel window, in decorated style. It was built as the office of the Leicester Water Company which was transferred to the Borough Corporation in 1878: until recently it was used as a Juvenile Court.

Facing us across Belvoir Street is the building affectionately known as the **PORK PIE CHAPEL** from its circular shape. Built as the United Baptist Church in 1842 at a cost of £9,000, it became redundant in 1939 and its congregation was merged with that of the Charles Street Baptist Church. It now forms part of the College of Adult Education. Its designer was Joseph Hansom of Hinckley, architect and inventor - he invented the Hansom cab which became so popular in the pre-motorcar era. As is so common with revolutionary introductions, though the cab was his idea, he failed to make a fortune from it for he was paid only £300 for his invention. He does not appear to have been a good businessman for when he designed Birmingham

City Hall in the style of the Parthenon his quotation was so low that he went bankrupt.

We turn right into Belvoir Street: **FENWICK'S STORE**, whose main entrance on the corner of Market Street is supported by a massive granite pillar, was built for Joseph Johnson & Company in 1880. To secure a position as a shop assistant with the latter company girls had first to serve an apprenticeship and were housed in the Crescent in King Street. The **CENTRAL LIBRARY** is on the corner of **WELLINGTON STREET**. This very finely proportioned building was designed by William Flint and built in 1831 by the Liberals, who were not allowed to meet in the Town Hall (the present Guildhall) which was at that time a Tory stronghold. At first it was called the 'New Hall', then the 'Wellington' or the 'Green Rooms' - an illusion to the Liberal party colour. The hall was used as a public lecture hall, a concert hall and a Liberal Club. The upper room housed the Leicester Mechanics Institute until it closed in 1870. Until 1848 it was the meeting place of the Leicester Literary and Philosophical Society. The Society's collection of 'natural and interesting objects' was kept there until it was presented to the town as the nucleus of the new Museum in New Walk. The Corporation purchased the hall for £3,160 in 1869 and two years later adapted it for use as a Municipal Free Library. It is said to be haunted.

On the left, as we look down Wellington Street, we see in the distance the offices of the Midland Bank which stand on the site of the workshop of **JAMES COOK** (we mentioned him on our first armchair tour when referred to the gibbet at the Guildhall). He was not related to Thomas Cook of travel fame. James was a book-binder and one day in May 1832, John Paas, a tool-maker and engraver, called on him to try to get an order. That night neighbours noticed that Cook's chimney was on fire: they broke into the building and found the fire out of control in the grate, with a hunk of meat on it. Cook was fetched from his home in Wheat Street; the fire was put out and Cook said that he had bought the meat for his dog but it had gone off so he decided to burn it. No one in authority could be called out at that time and he was allowed to go home, but when surgeons examined the meat on the next morning they declared that it was the seat, thigh bones and pelvis of a human being - all that remained of John Paas!

Cook fled during the night. He walked to Loughborough where he boarded the stage coach to Manchester and then another to Liverpool where he hoped to embark on a ship sailing to America. As he was being rowed out to such a ship his pursuers caught up with him; he dived overboard and swam ashore where he took a dose of laudanum in an unsuccessful attempt to commit suicide. His captors brought him back to Leicester to stand trial. He pleaded guilty and explained that he had owed John Paas twelve shillings and, to dispose of the debt, he killed him by hitting him on the head with an iron bar. He cut up the body with a saw and a cleaver and hoped to dispose of it by burning it on the fire. Cook was condemned to death and hanged in front of the Welford Road gaol before a crowd of 30,000, after which his body was gibbeted - the last one to be so treated in England.

Where Wellington Street and King Street come together in V-formation there stands a black and white mock-Tudor building erected in 1930 on the site of Thomas Cook's earlier travel office. The present building is the social club of the City Council employees. Across the road, on the corner of **KING STREET** and **WELFORD PLACE,** is **PHOENIX HOUSE**, built in 1842 to a design by William Flint, as the office of the Leicestershire & Midland Counties Fire and Life Insurance Company. As was common in those days, the company had its own fire station on the left hand side of the building opening onto Welford Place. Only two years later the bank which backed the Fire Office collapsed; the insurance company was dissolved and taken over by the Sun Fire Office. In 1866 the owner sold the building to Samuel Stone, a solicitor and for many years the Town Clerk. He compiled Stone's Justices' Manual - a reference book still published for the guidance of magistrates. The rear of Phoenix House was demolished some years ago and re-built. Fortunately the façade, with its fluted columns and ionic capitals, was preserved. In the seventeenth century there was a kiln in what is now Welford Place: bricks were made here for the restoration of the Castle in 1695.

Two hundred yards or so along King Street brings us to the bottom of **NEW WALK**. This pedestrian thoroughfare is unique - there is not another one like it anywhere in the country. It is three quarters of a mile long and was laid out in 1785 and followed the line of the Roman Via Devana, the Gartree Road, which came from Camulodunam near Colchester, through Ratae Corieltauvorum, Leicester's predecessor, to Deva - now Chester. New Walk was made to provide an alternative route from the town to the Race Course, on what is now Victoria Park. At that time Leicester was very small with only around 17,000 inhabitants. At first it was called Queen's Walk, after Queen Charlotte, the wife of King George III; then it became the Ladies' Walk and finally New Walk. Its construction was paid for out of public funds but an appeal raised £250 which paid for the trees which were planted to beautify the promenade: no doubt some of the magnificent specimens standing today are survivors from those originally planted.

New Walk ran along the edge of the **SOUTH FIELD** which was known as the Cowhay in medieval times: it was part of the Town Fields or common land. In 1630 these had an area totalling 2,800 acres, almost wholly unenclosed. By 1785 all had been enclosed except the 600 acre South Field and the Borough Corporation wanted to enclose that too to obtain higher rents by dividing the land into separate farms. To enable them to do this they had to reach agreement with the Freemen of the Borough.

The **FREEMEN OF THE BOROUGH OF LEICESTER** originally had to be sons of Freemen or to have served a seven year apprenticeship (referred to as 'servitude') or to have paid a sum of money (£35 in 1835). Women could not become Freemen. Freemen were permitted to trade in the town and to vote in parliamentary elections. In addition they had grazing rights for their livestock on the town fields, including the South Field.

The Act of Parliament sanctioning enclosure was passed in 1804; agreement was reached with the Freemen in 1811 and the land was finally enclosed in that year, after considerable resistance. Under the agreement the Freemen gave up their grazing rights and were given the freehold of 125 acres of the South Field, which became known as 'Freemen's Common: the Borough Corporation took the remainder. Freemen's Common is now an industrial estate north of Aylestone Road: the last six acres of it were sold to the Leicester Corporation in 1967 for £57,000 and the proceeds used to build sheltered housing known as 'Freemen's Holt' in Aylestone.

The enclosure of the South Field was a considerable financial success and it became possible to increase the salary of the part-time Town Clerk, William Heyrick, from £16. 13s. 4d., at which it had stood for 100 years, to £200. It also made it possible to develop New Walk and the series of public buildings and institutions on the upper slopes of the ridge. Wellington Street, parallel to New Walk in the east, and King Street, named after George III, cutting diagonally across it, were laid out in 1815; followed by Princess Road, then called Prince's Street, and Regent Road, named after the Prince Regent.

Prior to the enclosure New Walk was entirely rural in character. For several years there were no buildings on either side and it was an open promenade until 1824. Development was piecemeal with no overall plan: it was the practice to sell plots of land for building rather than developing and selling houses. A builder would buy a plot of land, build perhaps a pair of houses and had to sell them before he could buy more ground. In the mid-nineteenth century New Walk was largely middle class in character. Houses on the left side had back entrances reached from London Road. Carriages were only allowed to approach their owners' houses from the rear where there was stabling. Nowadays most of the properties are used for business purposes.

Let us walk up New Walk and look at the many and varied types of buildings: some are good original structures, others have been rebuilt and are out of character and disappointing, while many have been rebuilt and blend in very well with earlier buildings.

On the left is No.6B, built in 1880 as the **SUNDAY SCHOOL CENTENARY HALL**, with its projecting semi-octagon porch surmounted by an oriel window. Robert Raikes was one of the pioneers of the Sunday School movement, founded in 1780 to give a general education to poor children, and James Tait accepted no fee for designing this building which celebrated 100 years of progress. The inscription on the porch has been chipped away and after being used as a night club, the hall is in rather a dilapidated state.

Holy Cross Church and Blackfriars Hall. *(Leicester City Council)*

The first part of **HOLY CROSS CHURCH** was built in 1819, extended in 1886 and the newest part was added in 1956-58. The building opposite was opened as the **ROMAN CATHOLIC SCHOOL** in 1886. The words 'Boys' and 'Girls' can just be detected over the two doorways where they have been chiselled away. In recent years the school was converted into a Sikh Temple, which has been severely damaged by fire, and the building stands in a ruinous state. In the 1840's J. P. Clarke, a cotton reel manufacturer, built the **TEPID BATHS** on this site. In those days there were problems from smoke-pollution from factory chimneys and a stoker was liable to be fined 5s. and the owner 40s. for creating more than ten minutes smoke. J. P. Clarke had to dispose of large quantities of damp wood shavings on his furnace and threatened to close his works employing over 200 people if not allowed to do so. He solved the problem by advertising his chippings for fuel. He had a knack of using industrial waste and used the surplus hot water from his works for heating his private swimming baths which had entrances from New Walk and King Street. In 1847 the Corporation agreed to pay £100 a year towards his expenses. The public paid one penny admission charge which included the provision of a clean towel. In 1869 the Corporation decided to rent the baths entirely at a rental of £500 per year. This enabled children from the Union (Workhouse) to be admitted for a halfpenny, provided that they brought their own towel. The baths were fed by spring water which was constantly flowing at the rate of 9,000 gallons per hour. There was a large bath 100 feet long and 3 to 4 feet deep and a private bath 24 feet square. The Tepid Baths were closed in 1879 and new baths were opened in Bath Lane two years later.

The oldest part of the **NEW WALK MUSEUM** on the right hand side of New Walk, with its front looking like a Greek temple with its four massive Tuscan columns, was designed by Joseph Hansom and built in 1837 as the Nonconformist Proprietary School. The Anglican Collegiate School had been opened in College Street in 1836 and the Nonconformists feared 'lest the whole population should go bodily to Rome via Collegiate School', and resolved to found a school of their own. (The Collegiate School was closed in 1866 being unable to pay its way). The Proprietary School was never successful; it attracted few pupils and was soon in financial difficulties. The Borough Corporation purchased the site for £4,300 when it was closed down in 1847. It became a museum two years later when the Leicester Literary and Philosophical Society presented its collections to the municipality as a nucleus. The museum's lecture hall and art gallery were built in 1876 at a cost of £9,600.

In 1907 the British Association for the Advancement of Science held its first meeting in Leicester attended by 2,500 scientists. To entertain them a loggia was constructed in Museum Square, to the right of the former school building. The loggia's four sides provided a promenade 500 feet long and 25 feet wide. The external walls were closed and the internal wall looked on to a lawn 90 feet square. Around the walls a continuous buffet was arranged for the use of the delegates with a profusion of flowers provided by the Parks Department, while an orchestra provided music. The loggia was such a success that a campaign ensued to build a new public hall in Leicester. The result was the building of the De Montfort Hall in 1913.

New Walk Museum
(Leicester City Council)

The attractively designed houses opposite the Museum were built between 1825 and 1828 and have recently been restored. We cross the bridge over the Waterloo Way underpass and note the former **ST JOHN THE DIVINE CHURCH** in the distance to the left. The church was built in 1854 and designed by Sir George Gilbert Scott. It became redundant when most of the parishioners had moved away and was sold and converted into 38 flats. The church's ten bells were sold in 1983 to Peterborough Cathedral for £7,000.

Facing De Montfort Street, at the top of De Montfort Square, is the 9ft. tall white Sicilian marble statue of the **REVEREND ROBERT HALL**, standing on a 12ft. high Cornish granite pedestal. He is commemorated by a statue for the work he did trying to improve the lot of the framework knitters. He was born in Arnesby in 1764 and preached at the Particular Baptist Church in Harvey Lane, - the Holiday Inn stands on the site. In 1819, in a fight for a decent livelihood, he formed a relief committee to maintain framework knitters thrown out of work. He moved to Bath in 1826 and died there five years later. His statue was sculpted by John Birnie Philip who carved half the podium of the Albert Memorial in London. He is also commemorated by Robert Hall Baptist Church in Narborough Road.

The **BELMONT HOUSE HOTEL** stands on the New Walk/De Montfort Street corner. It was built in 1853 by William Rushin, builder of many New Walk properties including De Montfort Square, as Belmont House, a private girls' boarding and day school owned by Mrs. Catherine Schneider. Mrs. Schneider, who married her German master, and her sister Eliza came as the Misses Stringer, from Mount School, York - a Quaker school. Belmont House ceased to be a school in 1893. Since it became an hotel it has been extended several times and additional accommodation was built in 1990.

ST. STEPHENS UNITED REFORMED CHURCH stands on the opposite corner. Before the churches were amalgamated it was St. Stephens Presbyterian Church. It was originally built in 1869 on the corner of London Road and Station Street. Only fourteen years later it was demolished and removed stone by stone and re-erected on its present site.

Continuing up New Walk we turn into **THE OVAL** on the right and pass the former **COUNTY RECORD OFFICE** at 57 New Walk. Official records of the city and county, including Rutland, were preserved here. The premises, which used to be a house, became quite inadequate and were moved to more commodious accommodation at Wigston in 1992.

We reach **UNIVERSITY ROAD** which used to be called Victoria Road though on maps towards the end of the nineteenth century it is shown as Occupation Road. The section of pedestrian promenade before us is known as **UPPER NEW WALK**. Here the houses have their own consistent design which is different from the rest of New Walk. Some are very attractive and most date from the 1880s and reflect the increased prosperity of the people who built them. Most are now used for business or professional purposes. We turn right and go along University Road until we meet **REGENT ROAD**. The nurseries where most of the plants are grown for the attractive De Montfort Hall gardens are a little further along University Road on the left.

Another right turn takes us into **REGENT ROAD**. The older part, from Welford Road to De Montfort Street, was called Regent Street after the Prince Regent, later George IV, received representatives of the town at Belvoir in 1814. The newer part, laid out in the 1870s, was called Regent Road and this name was applied to the whole street around 1892.

As we go down Regent Road on the left we see the underground air-raid shelters made at the beginning of World War II, in the corner of what was the **WYGGESTON GIRLS' SCHOOL** playing field. These are sometimes used by the Fire Brigade for breathing apparatus practice. The school was founded in 1878 and opened with 150 pupils under its first headmistress Miss Ellen Leicester, taking its name from William Wyggeston, one of Leicester's benefactors. The present building was designed by Symington, Prince and Pike and built in 1926. In 1978 the school became **WYGGESTON COLLEGIATE SIXTH FORM COLLEGE**.

Three houses in Regent Road are interesting: the one on the corner of Salisbury Road was designed and lived in by Robert Johnson Goodacre. (He was a relative of John Johnson who designed the City Rooms). This house has a roof of American slates - imported as ballast. Number 86 Regent Road (it is now number 100), was the home of John Flower the artist who drew many scenes of Leicester as he saw it in the 1830s. This house was designed by him with Henry Goddard, father of the architect of the Clock Tower, and built in 1851. John Flower's initials appear on the front. The St. John Ambulance Headquarters, built in 1887, was the home of Henry Hughes and the motif HH (his initials) appears over fifty times in the brickwork!

This part of the South Field was a source of clay which was of suitable quality for brick-making. Lancaster Road, running parallel to Regent Road, used to be called Brick Kiln Lane. The headquarters of **EAST MIDLANDS GAS** on the De Montfort Street/Regent Road corner are built on the site of a former brickyard. The tower on the roof of the offices is part of a telemetric system which automatically regulates the flow of gas in the gas grid. The central fire station surrounded by firemen's houses, and its tower, can be seen down De Montfort Street. In the distance we can glimpse all that remains of the old power station, now redundant, built near that fragment of the Roman aqueduct called the Raw Dykes. South Fields College can also be seen: it provides courses on catering, hair-dressing, building and community care. The Cattle Market clock tower still gives us the time though the market has been closed down, and the new buildings of the Royal Infirmary, opened in 1978, feature prominently. This hospital was founded in 1771 by the Reverend Dr. William Watts and built on the site of

St. Sepulchre's Church. People who had been hanged were buried in the churchyard in what was called the Gallows Field.

Crossing the bridge over the main railway line to St. Pancras, the former **FIELDING JOHNSON HOSPITAL** is on our right. It consists of three houses built in Georgian style in 1844. In 1925 Paget Fielding Johnson bought and linked the houses together to form a single building and opened it as the Fielding Johnson Private Hospital - named after his father Thomas Fielding Johnson Junior. When the National Health Service came into being in 1948 it became an annexe to the Royal Infirmary, retaining some private beds. It was closed in June 1989 and it is planned to convert it into commercial premises.

The walls of **LEICESTER PRISON** with their television cameras can be seen on the left down **NEWTOWN STREET**; they are reputed to be the highest prison walls in the country. It is said that only one prisoner has ever escaped over them and he broke both legs! The prison, designed by William Parsons, was built in 1825-28. The entrance resembles one of Edward I's castles in North Wales and visitors sometimes think it really is a castle and have been known to enquire what the opening hours are! Public executions on a temporary scaffold used to take place in front of the prison - patients at the Infirmary opposite would line the windows to watch! The last public hanging in Leicester took place here in 1856 when William Brown, known as Peppermint Billy (his father made peppermints), was executed before a crowd of 25,000 spectators. He came from Scalford, near Melton Mowbray, and had been found guilty of murdering Edward and James Woodcock at Thorpe Toll Bar. Newtown Street was called Lower King Street until 1843 when it was given its present name - the 'new town' was the newly developed suburb of Southfields.

Leicester Prison
(J. W. Banner)

Passing the red brick buildings on the right of this part of Regent Road, which form residential accommodation for De Montfort University, we reach **HOLY TRINITY CHURCH** on the left. The first church on this site, designed by Sidney Smirke, was built in 1838 in a classical design wholly in keeping with other buildings in the street. The design became unfashionable and the building was Gothicised by S. S. Teulon in 1871 when he clad the Regency box-like structure in bluish-purple brick and built a huge steeple, bristling with details and flanked by two French pavilion roofs, forming an impressive back-drop to King Street. The fortunes of the church appear to have fluctuated: at one time, with a fall in the congregation, it became too large and part of it was made into a church hall; then in 1988-89 it apparently flourished again and had to be extended.

In **UPPER KING STREET** to the left are some splendid Regency houses, one of which used to be Holy Trinity Vicarage. Some years ago Regency Buildings, built in 1835, were beautifully restored and extended in the same style. Some of the houses bear a honeysuckle motif, a trademark of **WILLIAM FLINT** their architect who lived in King Street. He was responsible for **CRESCENT COTTAGES**. The end house of this terrace, on the corner of **KING STREET**, is now the office of an architect. This well preserved gem of the period was built in stuccoed brick in 1836. King Street was laid out between 1811 and 1813: it used to be fashionable to live there but when residents became prosperous and transport and roads improved, they moved out and used the sites of their houses to build factories.

On the other side of the street facing this Regency terrace is another Regency building, the sweeping and imposing **CRESCENT**. William Firmadge designed it in 1826 as a terrace of sixteen houses. Some years ago a planned ring-road put the Crescent in danger of demolition: fortunately the plan was dropped and in 1968 the terrace was excellently refurbished and converted into nine suites of offices. The Princess Road West/King Street corner was built in 1978 with old bricks and Swithland slates to blend perfectly with the Crescent. It was here, in the centre of the arc, that James Rawson set up the single remaining pillar of the old High Cross when it was taken down from the corner of High Street and Highcross Street in 1836.

A little way along King Street on the right, opposite **MARQUIS STREET**, was the home of Mrs. Hannah Cramant, a 'schoolmistress', and her five children. An opening, bridged over by the first floor of her home, led to **CRAMANT'S YARD**, a terrace of little back-to-back houses (without rear doors or windows), built in the 1820s. Twenty two people lived there in 1841 according to that year's census. Henry Taylor, a framework knitter, lived at no. 5 with his wife and seven children: space might have had to be found for a bulky knitting machine as well. While almost all Leicester's slum dwellings had been demolished in the first half of the nineteenth century, this yard survived in a dilapidated, unoccupied state. In recent years it has

The Crescent *(Leicester City Council)*

been restored and converted into office accommodation and is an interesting relic from the past.

Marquis Street was probably given that name because the famous general was created Marquis Wellington in 1812. **MARLBOROUGH STREET** on the left is only indirectly named after that famous soldier, the Duke of Marlborough. In 1828 it was called Union Place; by 1837 it had acquired its present name which was derived from a public house, Marlborough's Head. The well designed Victorian factory on the corner of Marlborough Street, the work of William Flint, was built in the mid-nineteenth century for hosier Richard Harris. It later became the factory of Pool, Lorrimer & Tabberer and part has now been converted into small industrial units by the City Council.

We pass the towering blocks of the **NEW WALK CENTRE**, speculatively built in 1971 to the design of Newman, Levinson & Partners on the site of the offices of the Wolsey knitwear company. The Centre was purchased by the City Council for £6m to consolidate their administrative offices which had been scattered over various sites in the city centre. We turn left into **LOWER NEW WALK**, cut off from New Walk by King Street, and go forward into **WELFORD PLACE**.

On its island site, the statue of **JOHN BIGGS** is a prominent feature of this busy area. His father was a framework knitter at a time when knitting was Leicester's only industry. John was born in 1801 and he and his brother William worked as winding boys for their father. It was common practice for a knitter to rent a frame and set it up in his own cottage. Mr. Biggs senior prospered and set up in a modest way as a hosier, renting frames to other knitters, supplying them with yarn to knit up into stockings and collecting the finished hosiery from them. He died in 1827 and his two sons continued the business. They were members of the Great Meeting, the Bond Street Unitarian Church, so influential in Leicester in the nineteenth century. They joined the Liberal party and became part of its radical wing. As young men, they were active in the drive for parliamentary reform which culminated in the passing of the Parliamentary Reform Act of 1832. They pressed for other reforms - the end of church tithes; the repeal of the Test Act which prevented dissenters from holding public office (it was repealed in 1828); the abolition of slavery and the repeal of the Corn Laws. They were active too in municipal reform: no municipal elections had every been held - the Borough Corporation was an oligarchy; existing members filled any vacancies as they occurred. The Municipal Reform Act was passed in 1835 and the old Tory Borough Corporation was thrown out at the first election in 1836, giving way to a new generation of Liberal reformers, including the Biggs brothers.

John concentrated on building up the family business - at one time they owned nearly a thousand stocking frames. William was more concerned with public life but had a breakdown and had to drop out for some years and John then came to the fore. Each brother was Mayor of Leicester three times and was returned to Parliament three times. Unfortunately the family firm collapsed in 1861, probably due to the time the brothers spent in their political and reforming activities. This marked the end of John Biggs's career in Leicester.

The Biggs family was active in everything relating to the welfare of the town. In 1850, at the instigation of John, 'flies' began to stand for hire in the streets. 'Fly' was a shortening of 'fly-by-night': these conveyances had previously been used mainly by ladies, who booked them in advance, for evening visiting. They gradually replaced sedan chairs and were at first drawn by a man and later by a pony or horse.

John Biggs built a large house in Knighton Park Road (now demolished). Having lost all his money in 1861, he went to live in a small house in Lancaster Road overlooking Nelson Mandela Park, where he died in poverty in 1871. His statue, sculpted by G. A. Lawson, was originally made of Sicilian marble and stands on a pedestal of Shap Fell granite. It was paid for by the contributions of over a thousand working people, showing their appreciation of his efforts on their behalf throughout his lifetime. After being damaged by a tramcar in 1928 it was repaired, and Joseph Herbert Morcom made a copy of the original in bronze which was installed on the pedestal in 1930.

Forming a back-drop to the statue is the great bowed front of the **LEICESTERSHIRE CLUB**, designed in Flemish style by Joseph Goddard and opened in 1873 at a cost of £8,000. It has excellent views down Welford Road to the prison. After being there for 117 years the club planned to vacate its premises in December 1990 and the building was offered for sale at £485,000, but arrangements were made by which a move to a new building was avoided.

The Queen Anne style factory on the corner of Newarke Street and Pocklington's Walk, built for Downings in 1881 and more recently occupied by the Central Institute which became a part of South Fields College in 1970, was pulled down in 1989. It has been replaced by magistrates courts which also extend along much of the left hand side of **POCKLINGTON'S WALK**. This street was cut through the garden of John Pocklington, a cattle auctioneer and Freeman of Leicester. He had been dismissed from the Town Council in 1766 for insolvency, but recovered from his financial problems and became Mayor in 1788. Unfortunately the mayoralty proved to be expensive and in 1789 he was only able to pay 11s. 3d. in the pound of the debt of £20 owing to Trinity Hospital. He died a poor man - a pensioner of the Corporation.

CHANCERY STREET on the left was called Catherine Street in 1828, after Catherine of Braganza, consort of Charles II. Nine years later the name was changed to its present form. The design of the **REGISTRY OFFICE**, farther along on the same side, was the result of a competition won by Redfern and Sawday in 1883. It was built as Poor Law Offices in Italian

style with Venetian windows and Corinthian capitals. The
CONSTITUTIONAL CLUB on the corner was restored a few years ago and converted into a Crown Court. It became redundant for that purpose when new Crown Courts were built near Waterloo Way in the 1980s, and is now a Careers Centre.

BERRIDGE STREET, facing us across Horsefair Street, was named after the family which owned the land when it was laid out in 1870-75. Turning right we pass the pedestrianized portion of Hotel Street on the left and Market Street on the right, and end our fourth armchair tour where we began on the corner of Bowling Green Street.

OUT AND ABOUT IN LEICESTER
CHAPTER FIVE

ROUTE:
Granby Street, London Road, Victoria Park, University, University Road, Welford Road, Almond Road, Aylestone Road, Infirmary Road, Oxford Street, Newarke Street.

STARTING PLACE:
Rutland Street/ Granby Street corner

Granby Street 1914
(Leicester City Council)

Granby Street 1950
(Leicester City Council)

Our fifth armchair tour begins on the corner of Granby and Rutland Streets and takes us in a southerly direction first along **GRANBY STREET**. On the left we pass **BALMORAL HOUSE**, designed by Shenton & Baker, built as a shoe factory in 1873. In the second half of the nineteenth century boot and shoe manufacture was becoming as important as the hosiery industry in Leicester. While there were a number of large concerns, small firms predominated: only a little capital was needed to set up in business, since all the machinery could be hired. The normal firm was a small family unit, managed by the proprietor with other members of his family. Balmoral House was a small factory of this kind and is typical of the way small businesses existed alongside shops and houses. It was built for Brewin & Sons and is currently occupied by a double-glazing company.

CHATHAM STREET on the other side of Granby Street was laid out around 1811 and named after the second Earl of Chatham. **YORK STREET** commemorates the Duke of York, (1763-1827), George III's second son, who was Commander-in-Chief of the British Army between 1798 and 1809. **DOVER STREET** and **CALAIS HILL** take their names from the Cross-Channel ports.

Still standing on this side is the former **TEMPERANCE HOTEL** now a shop retailing camping requisites. The hotel was opened in 1853 by Thomas Cook, and was managed by Marianne, his wife. She was Marianne Mason, a farmer's daughter: they met in 1827 when she was living at West Farm, Barrowden, and were married in 1833. The **TEMPERANCE HALL**, also owned by Thomas Cook, was next door to the hotel. He was a great advocate of temperance who believed in "taking the war to the enemy" and the Temperance Hall and the hotel were built between the Nag's Head and the

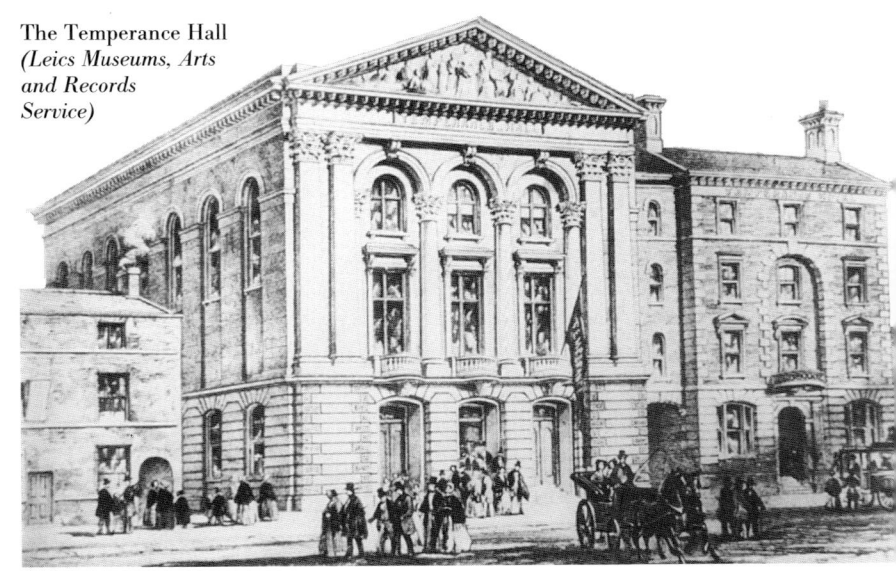

The Temperance Hall
(Leics Museums, Arts and Records Service)

Waggon & Horses! Many famous singers, including Jenny Lind, sang in the hall which was the town's leading public hall of any size until the De Montfort Hall was built in 1913. It eventually became the Essoldo Cinema which was demolished in 1961 along with one of Leicester's best known hosiery mills, the Britannia Works. Part of the site is now occupied by the Overseas Branch of the Midland Bank. The two public houses have gone but the Barley Mow still carries on the licensed trade.

The Leicester branch of the **YOUNG MEN'S CHRISTIAN ASSOCIATION** was flourishing with over 600 members at the beginning of the twentieth century when its very substantial new premises, at the end of Granby Street, were built to the design of A. E. Sawday - who was to become Mayor of Leicester in 1903 - in conjunction with Draper and Tudor Walters. It is constructed in the Baroque Style popular in the 1890s and 1900s, mainly of Ketton stone with some Leicester brick, and decorated with many stone carvings and columns. It was opened by the Marquess of Northampton on 5th December 1901. In 1978 the exterior was cleaned and the interior remodelled. The flower shop on the corner used to be the Windsor Cafe belonging to the Leicester Coffee & Cocoa House Company.

We avoid the heavy traffic by using the pedestrian underpass beneath the junction of **CHARLES STREET** and **LONDON ROAD**. Having come to the surface let us face the direction we have come and survey a bustling scene in an anti-clockwise direction. **CAMPBELL STREET** is on our right: it was laid out in 1838-9 and named after Colin Campbell Macaulay, the Midland Counties Railway's solicitor. It was constructed as the approach road to the new railway station. This impressive structure, built in 1840 and designed by William Parsons, architect of Leicester's prison, had an entrance built like a Greek temple with a massive pediment supported by four great fluted columns. It was from this station that Thomas Cook ran his first railway excursion to Loughborough on 5th July 1841. At that time the station had only one platform: it proved to be quite inadequate and had to be replaced 52 years later by a much larger station. The columns salvaged from the old station were incorporated into a large factory on the corner of Rolleston Street and Leicester Street but have now disappeared. Nowadays the **POST OFFICE** has a modern sorting office on the station site, handling mail from as far afield as Northampton. This is linked to the railway station and by a bridge across Campbell street to the parcels sorting office which adjoins the high-rise Post Office Leicester headquarters building on the St. George's Way/Campbell Street corner. British Telecom has its Leicester office here too.

The grey high-rise block of flats known as **ELIZABETH HOUSE,** designed by John Middleton, stands on our immediate right. This particular site has had a chequered history. In 1869 **ST. STEPHEN'S PRESBYTERIAN CHURCH** was built here and only 24 years later the site was sold for £10,000 and the church was taken down stone by stone and re-erected with several architectural improvements in its present position on the corner of New Walk and De Montfort Street: it is now a United Reformed Church. Thomas Cook then built his **WYVERN HOTEL** on the former church site: it was managed by his wife, Marianne. It was later converted into the **SHELL-MEX BUILDING** which had shops at street level including the Cafe Royal, one of J. S. Winn & Company's establishments, and a branch of Boots the Chemists. The building was pulled down in 1975 to make way for the present block of flats.

Continuing our anti-clockwise survey, before us is **ST. GEORGE'S WAY**, which takes its name from the nearby **ST. GEORGE'S CHURCH** - the first Anglican place of worship to be built in Leicester since the Reformation - now a Serbian Orthodox church. This road is part of the central ring road, it sweeps past the Post Office building passing the bottom of **SWAIN STREET**, a thoroughfare named after Alderman Robert Paddy Swain. He was a cigar manufacturer with business premises in what is now St. Nicholas Place. Iron gates bearing the letters S A & L, standing for Swain, Almond & Latchmore, secure the former factory's archway entrance to this day.

Looking to the left we catch a glimpse down **ST. GEORGE STREET** of the Leicester Mercury headquarters, opened by Princess Alexandra in 1966 - until then the newspaper's offices had been in Albion Street for 76 years. The land in the area of **NORTHAMPTON SQUARE** belonged to the Marquess of Northampton at one time and here stands the imposing **CENTRAL POLICE STATION**, built in 1933 to the design of Noel Hill. Older citizens will recall it being heavily protected by sandbags during World War II.

The original **CHARLES STREET** used to be a narrow thoroughfare, laid out around 1800, lined with terraced houses, running between Humberstone Gate and Northampton Square. It was named after King Charles II. Charles Street as we know it today was opened in 1932 as Leicester's 'million pound street'. It was created by cutting through into London Road, widening the old Charles Street and extending it from Humberstone Gate to Belgrave Gate. The dual carriageway was intended to take traffic away from the Clock Tower area and it was thought that this would become the city's principal shopping street. The central reservations between the carriageways used to be adorned by concrete troughs filled with flowers - nicknamed 'Beckett's buckets' after the City Engineer. Unfortunately fumes from traffic were too much for the plants and the troughs had to go.

We swing round visually past Granby Street which we have already seen, to **EAST STREET** which was given this name because it was in the eastern part of the South Field. To the left of the street are two huge blocks of office accommodation, Peat House and Arhem House, which were built in 1990. We have now turned the full circle and face up **LONDON ROAD**.

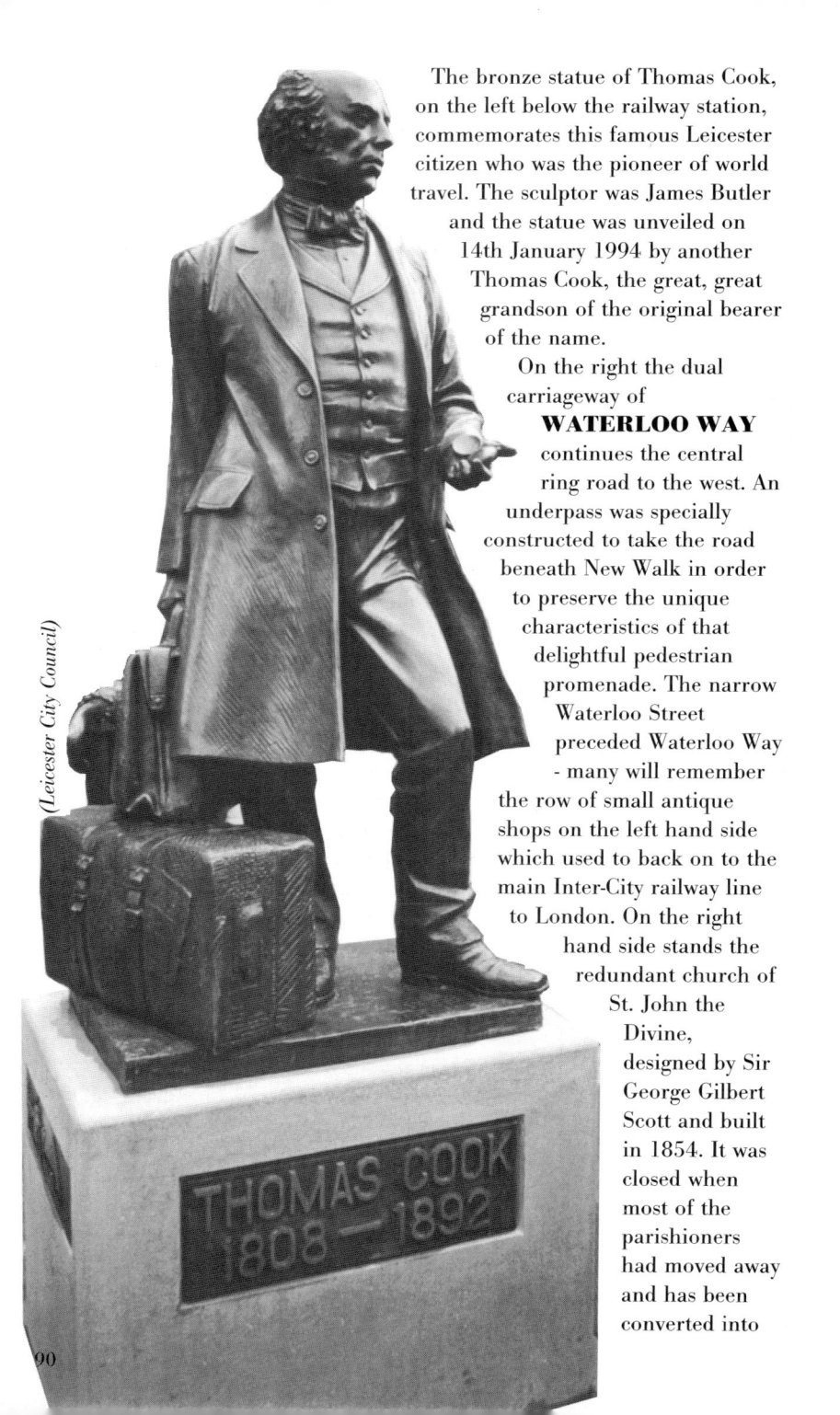

(Leicester City Council)

The bronze statue of Thomas Cook, on the left below the railway station, commemorates this famous Leicester citizen who was the pioneer of world travel. The sculptor was James Butler and the statue was unveiled on 14th January 1994 by another Thomas Cook, the great, great grandson of the original bearer of the name.

On the right the dual carriageway of **WATERLOO WAY** continues the central ring road to the west. An underpass was specially constructed to take the road beneath New Walk in order to preserve the unique characteristics of that delightful pedestrian promenade. The narrow Waterloo Street preceded Waterloo Way - many will remember the row of small antique shops on the left hand side which used to back on to the main Inter-City railway line to London. On the right hand side stands the redundant church of St. John the Divine, designed by Sir George Gilbert Scott and built in 1854. It was closed when most of the parishioners had moved away and has been converted into

38 flats, most of them incorporating some feature from the church such as a pillar capital or a stained glass window. The ten bells were sold for £7,000 in 1983 and have been hung in Peterborough Cathedral. Standing a little further along on the same side are the red brick Crown Courts, built around 1980.

The red brick and terracotta **RAILWAY STATION** on the left was designed by Charles Trubshaw, the Midland Railway Company's architect, and built in 1892 to replace the original Campbell Street station. St. Paul's Methodist New Connexion Chapel, built in 1861, had to be pulled down to make way for the station. The chapel was rebuilt in Melbourne Road and the four columns with Corinthian capitals which had fronted it went to a building in North Evington when London Road Station was built. The platform buildings have been completely rebuilt but the station entrance is to be preserved and has been thoroughly cleaned and restored.

The railway has played a considerable part in the industrial development of Leicester. John Ellis, a farmer at Beaumont Leys, with Robert Stephenson as engineer, was responsible for the construction of the Leicester and Swannington line in 1832, which meant cheaper coal for industrial and domestic use. The Midland Counties Railway followed and later, as the result of amalgamations with other lines, including the Leicester and Swannington railway in 1846, became the Midland Railway Company of which both John Ellis and his son Edward Shipley Ellis became chairmen.

The next street on the left is **CONDUIT STREET**. In 1612 the town's first supply of water was brought in a conduit of lead pipes from a spring in St. Margaret's Field down this street to what was also called the Conduit in the Market Place. **ARTHUR WAKERLEY**, the architect, lived at number 46 London Road (now number 58) for over twenty years. Number 64 was the home of **DR. WILLIAM JOHNSTON** (1845-1900): he had a surgery in the yard. Dr. Johnston was active in the eradication of smallpox and was a prolific campaigner at a time when many Leicester citizens were anti-vaccinationists. In 1872 he started a hospital, which eventually had 108 beds, on Freakes Ground on the corner of Fosse Road North and Groby Road, for the treatment of measles, smallpox, cholera and erysipelas, and in 1876 was appointed Assistant Medical Officer for Leicester. He is remembered as a very strong character, a fighter and a visionary.

PREBEND STREET runs parallel to Conduit Street. This area used to be in the parish of St. Margaret which was in a special position owing feudal allegiance to the Bishops of Lincoln, jurisdiction having been transferred to them when the Leicester Bishopric ceased in the 870s at the time of the Danish invasion. The church was a prebendal church of Lincoln Cathedral until 1878.

At the far end of Prebend Street, in **COLLEGE STREET**, what used to be the **COLLEGIATE SCHOOL** can be seen. This is the original building, built in Gothic style, and opened in 1836 as the private fee-paying

Anglican Boys' School. Unfortunately it was unable to pay its way and was closed in 1866. The building was sold for £4,000 for use as a Congregational Church. It later became the Collegiate Girls' School until that school was amalgamated with the Wyggeston Girls' School to become the Wyggeston Collegiate Sixth Form College. It is now to become the headquarters of the County Museums and Arts Service.. On the opposite side of London Road **REGENT STREET** was named after the Prince Regent, later George IV, and **NELSON STREET** commemorated the famous Admiral of the Napoleonic Wars. In this street the factory where Goddard's Plate Powder was made is interesting. Built in 1932, the walls have an art deco glass surface supported by thin aluminium bars. **DE MONTFORT STREET** takes its name from Simon de Montfort, Earl of Leicester, who is commemorated by a statue on the Clock Tower as one of Leicester's benefactors.

SAXBY STREET, on the left, was one of six streets which had their names changed in 1918 at the request of the inhabitants, as a result of World War I. There was opposition to anything so German sounding as its original name of Saxe-Coburg Street, named after the royal family. Andover Street, off Conduit Street, was another one of the six - it used to be Hanover Street, after the House of Hanover.

Opposite Saxby Street is a building rejoicing in the nickname of **TOP HAT TERRACE** which has an interesting story. When the Leicester police force was formed in 1836 its first detective was Francis 'Tanky' Smith. He and a second detective, Tommy Haynes (Black Tommy), did much to clear up the town's crime, breaking up gangs of thieves who infested the streets and alleyways. 'Tanky' was a master of disguise and was able to mingle with the criminal fraternity. He retired in 1864 and became Leicester's first private detective. He made a reputation for himself when he was hired by the Winstanley family of Braunstone Hall to look for James Beaumont Winstanley, the High Sheriff of the County, who was missing on a European tour. 'Tanky' traced him to Koblenz where his body was found floating in the River Moselle. He was richly rewarded and invested the

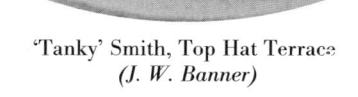

'Tanky' Smith, Top Hat Terrace (J. W. Banner)

money in land, building Victoria (Top Hat) Terrace and developing Francis Street in Stoneygate. Top Hat Terrace was designed by 'Tanky's' son, James Francis Smith: he incorporated sixteen carved stone heads each of them representing his father in one of his many disguises. One or two have been given a top hat - part of a policeman's uniform until 1872. The terrace was restored in 1987 with a grant of £7,700 from the City Council.

The original name of **UNIVERSITY ROAD** was Occupation Road. This was changed to Victoria Road in 1867, the year **VICTORIA ROAD CHURCH**, with its 120ft. spire, was opened. This was a Baptist church but the building now belongs to the Seventh Day Adventists. The street was re-named University Road in 1929 following the establishment of Leicester University as Leicester, Leicestershire & Rutland College in 1921. The **PARK HOTEL** on the De Montfort Street/University Road corner is the terminal building of a block that ran from New Walk to London Road, designed by James Francis Smith.

The streets of **HIGHFIELDS** were laid out in the grounds of Highfield House following the death in 1868 of its owner, Joseph Whetstone, but **HIGHFIELD STREET** which we come to next on the left, was in existence as early as 1857. Until improvement in public transport encouraged the extension of the town into what became known as Stoneygate, Highfields was a residential area favoured by prominent citizens, often manufacturers, who built houses for themselves and more modest dwellings for their workers.

Until the establishment of a stage coach service roads were little more than tracks used by carriers and postmen on horseback or on foot. In 1726 the first serious attempt to improve the roads was made when a Turnpike Act was passed for the most important road in the county, from Loughborough through Leicester to Market Harborough. The Borough Corporation borrowed £150 from Alderman Gabriel Newton to cover the expenses involved and secured substantial representation on the Turnpike Trust which was established to manage the roads and to administer the tolls which were levied. Apart from income from tolls, maintenance of this section of the turnpike had to be borne by the parishioners of St. Margaret's parish which extended as far as Victoria Park Road until the beginning of the nineteenth century. Two turnpike gates were set up on the approaches to the town, one at the bottom of Red Hill, Birstall, and the other nearly at the top of **LONDON ROAD** opposite where the Marquess Wellington public house stands today. The toll for horses was 4 $1/2$d. each, oxen were charged $1/2$d. and sheep $1/4$d. In 1851 tolls were paid on 80,000 horses, but the slope of the road was proving too steep for the increasing traffic and horses found it difficult to start up again having stopped at the toll gate. It became necessary to replace the toll bar by another one near the London Road end of Victoria Park Road. When tolls were finally ended the toll house was taken down and re-erected in Knighton Drive for use as a coachman's house and it is still there. Public passenger traffic did not begin until 1759 when a coach service was established from London to Leicester, Nottingham and Derby, three times a week, followed in 1765 by 'flying machines' travelling to London in a single day.

The substantial houses which lined both sides of London Road all had extensive front gardens but all have disappeared over the years with successive road widening schemes and all housing has been converted for business or professional use. **MILL HILL LANE,** opposite the Marquess Wellington, once led to a windmill at its eastern end. **EVINGTON ROAD,** as its name implies, is the road leading to the village of Evington, now incorporated into the city. When the crown of London Road, by the end of Evington Road, was being lowered in 1853, between one and two hundred skeletons were found. The discovery of Saxon brooches indicate that they may have been Saxons or Danes.

GRANVILLE ROAD opposite was named after the second Earl of Granville (1815-91), who was Foreign Secretary three times. The studio of Leicester Sound Radio, in a building designed by Thomas Barnard in 1875, is on the right hand side.

In earlier years the whole of the streets from the site of the Clock Tower, along Granby Street and London Road, as far as Victoria Park Road were collectively known as **GALLOWTREE GATE.** The road led to the gallows which were at the end of the Evington Footway at the top of the hill.

We now go through the gates into **VICTORIA PARK** one of Leicester's 'lungs'. In 1806 the **RACECOURSE** was moved to this open space from St. Mary's Field and a grandstand was built, which became the park pavilion when horse racing was transferred to the Oadby race course in 1884. The grandstand was destroyed by a parachute mine during an air-raid on 20th November 1940 and a new pavilion was built some years after the end of the War. The clock in the pavilion tower was provided in the will of John Ambrose Hartshorne of Leicester who died on 16th December 1953. The splendid wrought iron park gates, and a similar pair at the bottom of Peace Walk, were presented by Sir Jonathan North in 1931 in memory of Eliza, his wife. He served the town as Mayor for four years during World War I (1914-18). He was Chairman of Freeman, Hardy & Willis, at the time the largest firm of distributors in the British footwear trade. The two pavilions which flank the gates were erected in the same year and designed by Sir Edwin Lutyens.

After the Wharf Street cricket ground was sold for building purposes in 1860, **COUNTY CRICKET** was played on Victoria Park until 1873, the year in which the Leicester County Cricket Association was formed. The first **FOOTBALL** clubs date from 1869: in 1880 they united and played soccer and rugby in alternate weeks on a ground in Belgrave Road and on Victoria Park. Four years later the two games split apart. Leicester Fosse Football Club was formed to pursue soccer alone on their new ground in Filbert

Street, and Leicester Football Club (the Tigers, after their striped shirts), played rugger on their new ground in Welford Road. The park is widely used for both football, cricket and tennis in the various seasons.

As we walk along the roadway from the gates, set back a little and protected by a heavy iron fence, we see an oak tree of the variety *quercus roba*. An oak tree was planted here by Alderman Ernest Grimsley, Leicester's eighth Lord Mayor, on 6th May 1935 to commemorate King George V's Jubilee. Three oak trees altogether had been planted on different occasions to commemorate important events, including one planted by Alderman W. J. Lovell to celebrate the end of World War I. Alderman Grimsley's tree used to bear a plaque which disappeared years ago. In the evening after his planting a huge bonfire was lit followed by a fireworks display. It is probable that all these trees were destroyed by the parachute mine which demolished the old park pavilion during World War II.

To commemorate the visit to Leicester of King George VI and Queen Elizabeth on 30th October 1946, the Lord Mayor, Alderman Charles Worthington, accompanied by Vic Oliver, the comedian who married Winston Churchill's daughter, planted an oak tree on approximately the same site. This is the tree, surrounded by the iron fence, which is growing there today.

Near the Granville Road gate into the park there used to be a small drinking fountain with a bronze figure of Æthelfloeda in the centre. She was the Queen of Mercia and the daughter of King Alfred. She defended Leicester against the Danish onslaught and is said to have rebuilt the town

(Leicester City Council)

walls. The fountain was a memorial to Edith Gittins, artist and social reformer (1845-1910). As a member of the Leicester Womens's Liberal Association, she was a prime mover of the Leicester Women's Suffrage Society. When the bronze statue was stolen some years ago the fountain was removed to the Market Place and a replacement statue was made. After this had been stolen and recovered twice it was installed in the foyer of the City Rooms where it will be safe from vandalism.

The **GRANITE BOULDER** on the left was inaugurated in 1976 by United States General Matthew Ridgway, as Leicester's tribute to the memory of the men of the U.S. 82nd. Airborne Division who were stationed in and around the City prior to the D-Day invasion of Europe in 1944. The **MEMORIAL ARCH** built of Portland stone and designed by Sir Edwin Lutyens is a replica, though slightly smaller, of a similar memorial he designed for New Delhi, India. Standing on high ground, the arch was unveiled in 1925 and is a noble tribute to those men who fell in two World Wars. A stipulation was made that no higher buildings should be permitted in the vicinity.

We pass the **DE MONTFORT HALL,** with its beautiful gardens, on the right. Until 1913 the only public hall in Leicester was the Temperance Hall in Granby Street. Here the sale of liquor was not allowed and this, with other factors, limited its use and led to a campaign being mounted to encourage the building of a new hall. There was much grumbling - Victoria Park was out of the way, too far from the centre of the town, inconvenient and in entirely the wrong position. The campaigners won the day and a competition held to decide the best design was won by Shirley Harrison of Stockdale Harrison. A myth has long prevailed in Leicester that the De Montfort Hall was built as a temporary structure but it seems highly improbably that such a substantially constructed building should have been intended to be only temporary, especially bearing in mind that it cost the ratepayers £21,000, (around £^{1}/$_2$m. in today's money). It was opened on 21st July 1913. Its name presented a problem: at first it was called 'The Public Hall': the Mayor wanted to call it 'St. George's Hall' but this name was rejected, and finally its present name was agreed upon. When the foundations were being laid the sub-soil was found to be too soft for normal foundations and the hall had to be built on brick piers which might account for its wonderful acoustics. Little was known at that time about the science of acoustics and, when the Royal Festival Hall in London was to be built, it is said that its architects came to study the De Montfort Hall before they finalised their plans. Orchestral conductors from all over the world have praised the hall's acoustics as some of the finest they have encountered, and it is generally agreed that it is one of the finest concert halls in the Midlands and one of the best acoustically in England. It can seat 3,000 people, all with an unobstructed view. The organ was the gift of Alfred Corah: when it was inaugurated in 1914 he gave a recital to his own workpeople - employees of

N. Corah & Sons.

We continue along the path on the edge of the park and until we reach **PEACE WALK** which was known as the Processional Way when it was laid out at the time the memorial arch was built - the name was changed in 1981. It is most attractive when viewed from Sir Jonathon North's decorative pair of wrought iron gates at the bottom of the slope: it is planted with lovely flowers in spring and summer and the arch in the centre in the distance is most impressive.

The footpath from Victoria Park Road to the University is lined with eighty **OAK TREES** forming an avenue planted in 1980 to commemorate the eightieth birthday of Queen Elizabeth the Queen Mother.

From the park we can enter the campus of the **UNIVERSITY** on our right. Dr. Astley Clarke, a learned physician, played a major part in the beginnings of the University. After the armistice in 1918 he launched a public appeal for funds, which raised £100,000 for the establishment of a Leicester, Leicestershire and Rutland College to commemorate the war service of men of town and county. The 40 acres of land on which the University and the Wyggeston & Queen Elizabeth I Sixth Form College are now built, together with the old asylum, were purchased by Thomas Fielding Johnson, a worsted spinner, in 1919 for £40,000 and presented to the town for educational purposes: part of the site was allocated to the Wyggeston Boys' Grammar School, and the asylum and 9 acres were reserved for the College.

The College began in 1921 with nine students, three lecturers, a secretary and the Principal, Dr. R. F. Rattray, who was minister of Great Meeting Unitarian Church in Leicester. He taught English and Latin and the first lecturers taught French, geography and botany. Later further departments were added and the title was changed to Leicester University College in 1926. The College bought a further nine acres in University Road from the City Council in 1949 with a view to future developments. From these small beginnings the University was granted its charter as an independent university in 1957 and Lord Adrian became the first Chancellor. At that time 816 students were enrolled: today there are around 9,500, including post-graduate students and part-time undergraduates.

The University continued to expand and the chemistry laboratories were opened in 1959, a research building in 1960, and the physics building in 1961. The Law Faculty was added in 1975 together with the Faculty of Medicine which admitted its first students in that year. It had been preceded by the School of Biological Sciences, housed in the Adrian Building in 1967. The Bennett Building housed geology, geography and mathematics.

The **LEICESTERSHIRE AND RUTLAND LUNATIC ASYLUM** was built in 1837 at a cost of £18,000 to the design of William Parsons who was the architect of Leicester's Welford Road prison. At first the asylum housed 104 patients but by 1897, after many extensions, they totalled 606.

The inmates were responsible for cultivating 72 acres of farm land. The hospital was closed in 1910 when Carlton Hayes hospital was built. In 1915 it was transformed into the 5th Northern Military Hospital which, with temporary buildings on the hospital's farm, housed 1,750 beds. The building is now known as the **FIELDING JOHNSON BUILDING** and the accommodation is used to house the University's administration and the Faculty of Law. The bronze sculpture by Helaine Blumenfeld named 'Souls', in the middle of the lawn facing this building, was unveiled by the Vice Chancellor, Dr. Kenneth Edwards, in September 1990.

The **ENGINEERING BUILDING,** with its distinctive glass roof and high-rise tower, designed by Stirling and Gowan and erected in 1962, was hailed as an architectural masterpiece and featured on a postage stamp in 1967. Charles Wilson succeeded F. L. Attenborough as the third principal of Leicester University College in 1951. He became the University's first Vice-Chancellor when its charter was granted in 1957. The **CHARLES WILSON BUILDING** was named after him: it was designed by Denys Lasdun & Partners and opened in 1968. It is a social building incorporating a sports hall, coffee bar, restaurants and staff common rooms. Charles Wilson resigned the Vice-Chancellorship in 1961 to become Principal of Glasgow University and was knighted. He was succeeded by Sir Fraser Noble who was to become Principal of Aberdeen University in 1976.

The **ATTENBOROUGH BUILDING**, which is eighteen storeys high and has a block of lecture theatres in the rear, accommodates the Faculties of Arts and Social Sciences. It is named after F. L. Attenborough the

(Leicester City Council)

Welford Road Cemetery before the chapel was demolished in 1950s

University College's second principal; he was the father of Richard and David who have respectively achieved fame in films and television and who, as boys, lived in a house on the campus which still stands today.

    The University's **PERCY GEE BUILDING** was opened by the Queen in 1958 and is the headquarters of the Students' Union, with refectories, a shop, common rooms and a theatre. It was given its name in honour of the friend and benefactor who had been chairman of the University's Council since 1945. Percy Gee was a director of Stead & Simpson Ltd., one of the leading companies in Leicester's shoe industry. A feature of the **LIBRARY** is its glass front which reflects the towering Attenborough Building and the new Mathematics Building, built in 1990. The Library was built over the courtyard of the Fielding Johnson Building in 1974 and its facilities were extended in 1994 when the bookstore was built in Putney Road.

    The **BIOCENTRE** and the **COMPUTER CENTRE** are accommodated in a single building on the right, at the bottom of Mayors Walk. In the Biocentre genetic experiments are carried out in an effort to produce improved strains of plants which are also disease resistant. It was here that genetic 'finger-printing' was developed which has revolutionised crime detection and the establishment of paternity.

    We leave the campus passing first the front of the Fielding Johnson Building on the left, and then the **ASTLEY CLARKE BUILDING**, which houses the Faculty of Psychology on our right, and return to University Road. As we look back towards Regent Road we see the massive block of the **MEDICAL SCIENCES BUILDING** on the left, built on the site of the former Leicester Bowling Club's green and linked by a bridge over the road to the School of Biological Sciences, in the Adrian Building. These two buildings, together with the **CLINICAL BUILDING** at the Royal Infirmary, completed in 1978, constitute the University's School of Medicine.

    Passing along University Road we reach **WELFORD ROAD**. The area directly facing us used to be part of **FREEMEN'S COMMON**. After the Act of Parliament was passed in 1804, which permitted the Borough Corporation to enclose the South Field, agreement was reached with the Freemen of Leicester whereby they were granted the freehold of 125 acres, known as Freemen's Common, as compensation for their loss of grazing rights on the common land. A major part of this land is now occupied by the University's main car park and students' living quarters, but the old Freemen's Cottages, built as Alms Houses in 1855 and extended in 1890, still stand. They have been refurbished and adapted as a Medical Centre serving both the Leicester and De Montfort universities. Leicester University's Victorian Studies Centre was housed there for a time.

    Turning right and going a little way down the hill we come to the main entrance of the **WELFORD ROAD CEMETERY,** now closed for burials. This is the last resting place of many notable citizens and hundreds

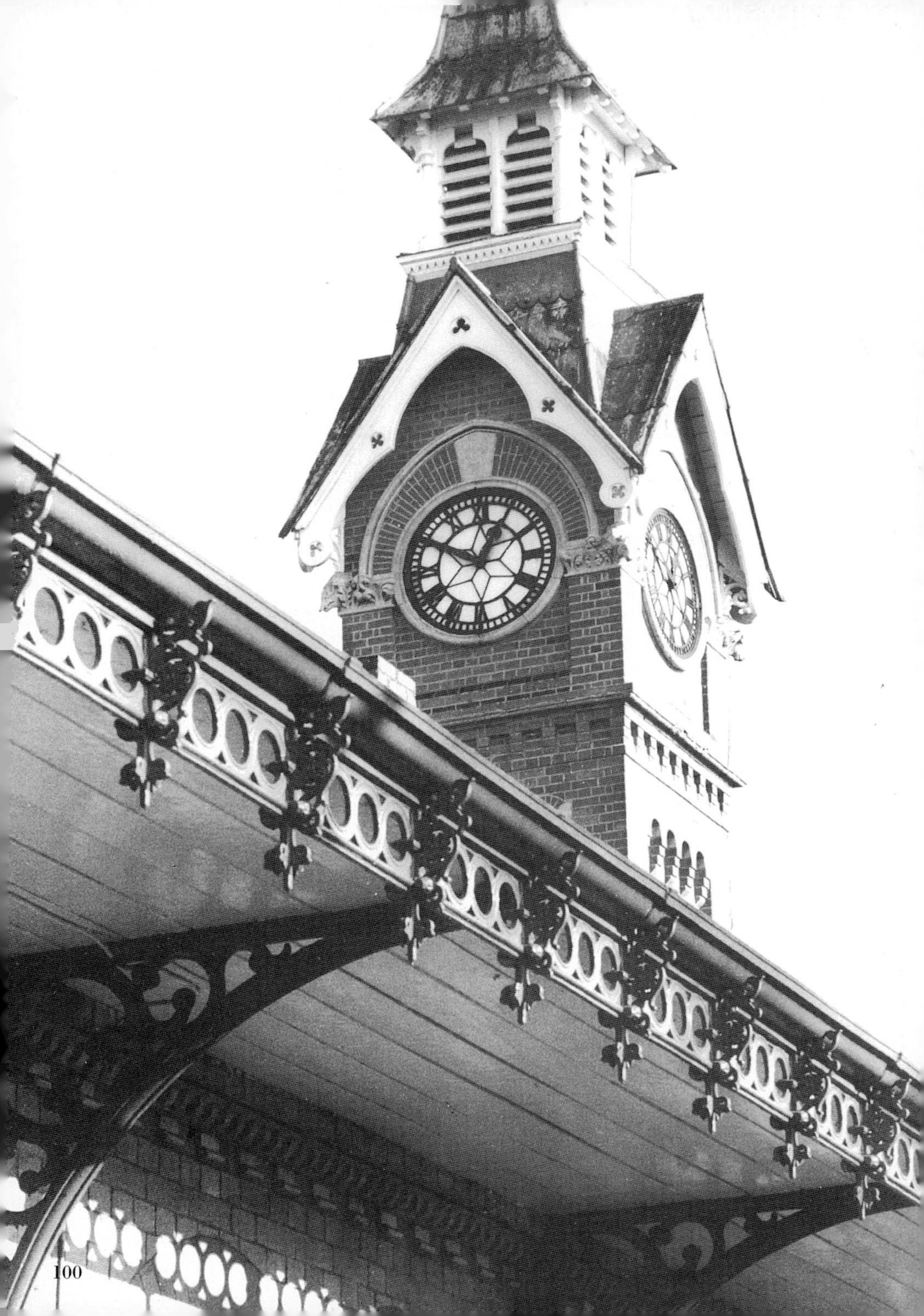

of less well known ones. An hour or two could be spent among the rows of splendidly sculpted Victorian memorials noting the names of well-known people. For example there is the grave of William Rushin who built many of the houses and the Belmont House school (now Hotel), in New Walk, but perhaps one of the most interesting is that belonging to the Cook family.

Marianne Cook, who ran Thomas's two hotels, is buried here along with their daughter Annie Elizabeth who died in tragic circumstances in 1880 at the age of 35, at their home, 'Thorncroft' on London Road, now the headquarters of Leicester Red Cross. She was drowned in the bath - probably asphyxiated by a defective gas water heater - one of the first victims of death by this cause. She wanted to marry one of her father's employees and, because he objected to the match, it was thought at first that she had committed suicide and an open verdict was brought in at the inquest. Thomas was devastated and had the dozens of letters of sympathy which were sent to him, bound in a leather-backed book which is preserved in the County Record Office. He set up the Annie Elizabeth Cook Memorial Trust which built the Memorial Hall bearing her name in Archdeacon Lane. It was associated with Archdeacon Lane Baptist Church where she ran the Sunday School. Both church and hall have gone - demolished to make way for the inner ring road. At the age of 84 Thomas died in 1892, by which time he was blind. When the Midland Bank, which then owned the travel company, had the memorial stone in the cemetery cleaned a few years ago, they installed a plaque which truthfully states that *'... he brought travel to the millions'*.

The building on the Welford Road/Almond Road corner used to be a mortuary and later a B.B.C. radio studio from which local reporters could phone in their stories and have them recorded. **ALMOND ROAD** was made in the 1970s when a new gyratory traffic system was created. It was evidently given this name as an addition to the other streets named after nuts in this district. Half way down on the left is an entrance to the former **CATTLE MARKET**. This market was moved from the Horsefair Leys (the present Town Hall Square) to this site on 6th April 1872. The buildings, dominated by the clock tower, were designed by J. B. Everard and built in the previous year at a cost of £27,615. The cattle market was closed on 8th December 1988. Four years before this the massive iron gates had been taken down and re-erected along the side of Aylestone Road where they serve a purely decorative function. The future of the cattle market site is uncertain.

SOUTH FIELDS COLLEGE, on the right hand side of Almond Road, was planned in the late 1960s and opened in this new building in September 1970. One of its constituent parts was the former Central Institute which offered courses for women and for caterers in the old Downing's factory building (now demolished) at the Welford Place end of Newarke Street. Among the courses provided in the new building are catering, bakery, community care and hair-dressing. The catering department has restaurants open to the public. The premises were greatly extended in 1982 and the building department was moved from Newarke Street. There are printing and footwear departments in other premises away from the central site.

If we look to the left when we reach the junction with **AYLESTONE ROAD,** in the distance on the right is the site of the former power station and **RAW DYKES ROAD**. This takes its name from the **RAW DYKES**, the Roman aqueduct, a section of which still remains: it carried water $1^{1}/_{4}$ miles from the Knighton Brook to the Roman Baths at the Jewry Wall. **ALL SOULS CHURCH** stands facing the College. It was built of red brick with limestone dressings in 1904-6, as a memorial to John and Sarah Nedham, by their daughters, costing them £10,000.

The next street on the left is another 'nut' street - **BRAZIL STREET** - then comes **SAWDAY STREET**, perhaps named after a Leicester architect bearing that name. Next is **FILBERT STREET**, renowned as the home of Leicester City Football Club, and running parallel to it, **WALNUT STREET**, the last of the 'nut' streets.

The **FOSSE CENTRE**, next door to South Fields College, is devoted to the welfare of people with learning difficulties. The ground of the **LEICESTER FOOTBALL CLUB**, the Rugby playing 'Tigers', comes next and then we reach the **GRANBY HALLS**. They were built as 'temporary' buildings in 1915 as the Junior Training Halls and were used during World War I for training purposes. Later they became exhibition halls - for some fifty years the Home Life Exhibition was held here every September - and were also used for roller skating and other functions. Now they have been made into a centre accommodating a multitude of leisure activities.

From the early seventeenth century horse racing was held on the Abbey Meadow but because of floods had to be moved in 1742 to a part of what was known as **ST MARY'S FIELD**: this was the land on which the Cattle Market, South Fields College and adjacent buildings, the Royal Infirmary and the housing in the 'nut' street area now stand. The race track was inconvenient because it had to cross the turnpike roads to Aylestone and Wigston, consequently the racecourse had to be moved again to what is now Victoria Park, in 1806.

We go forward into **INFIRMARY ROAD,** with the Welford Road recreation ground on our right - now re-named **NELSON MANDELA PARK,** and the high walls of the **PRISON** next to it, fronted by its castle-like entrance. The **ROYAL INFIRMARY** on the left was founded by the Reverend Dr. William Watts, Vicar of Medbourne. He lived at Danetts Hall which was in the Westcotes area of Leicester - a district long since built over. He launched an appeal and £2,500 was quickly raised enabling a site to be purchased in 1768. Plans for the hospital's earliest buildings, which had 60 beds and are still in use, were drawn up by Benjamin Wyatt and William

Henderson and the hospital was opened in 1771 and became at once the county's most widely supported charitable institution. A subscriber's order was required for every patient admitted and when it was laid down that hospital supplies must be bought from subscribers, Leicester tradesmen began to see the advantage in giving the hospital their financial support. The Infirmary - as it was then, it became 'Royal' in 1912 - was built on the site of the old St. Sepulchre's Church which was to the south of the medieval South Gate: criminals who had been hanged were buried in St. Sepulchre's churchyard. In the 1850s the Squire of Quenby Hall - a member of the Ashby family - gave the Hall's ornamental wrought iron gates to the Infirmary where they were erected. They now stand in the garden of the Newarke Houses Museum. In recent years the hospital has been greatly enlarged with the building of a maternity hospital, new wards, a new accident and outpatients department, and the University's Clinical Sciences Building. After recent extensions, the Royal Infirmary provides a comprehensive district general hospital of 1,250 beds. There is an interesting sculpture of healing hands supporting a sick woman attached to the wall of the former outpatients department: it was carved by A. Pountney in 1954.

We come to **PELHAM STREET** on the right, named after Henry Pelham Clinton, fourth Duke of Newcastle, and pass beneath the foot bridge which links the hospital to its multi-deck car park to reach **INFIRMARY SQUARE** on the left, from which Infirmary Close leads to the main entrance to the Royal Infirmary. Passing **CARLTON STREET** we continue into **OXFORD STREET** which used to be called Horsepool Street because there was a pool here for watering horses: it had been given its present name by 1826. **GRANGE LANE** on the left used to lead to the grange or farm belonging to Leicester Castle. Passing the huge white blocks of flats on the right, which are built on the site of Pickard's worsted spinning mill - note the old entrance arch which has been preserved - we come to **BONNERS LANE,** named after Robert Bonner who left property in Horsepool Street in 1763. His daughter kept the Duke of Rutland Inn in that street.

Bonners Lane runs into **MILL LANE** which once led to the Newarke Mill. **DE MONTFORT UNIVERSITY**, formerly Leicester Polytechnic, occupies the area bounded by these two streets, Oxford Street, the Newarke and the river, and has replaced many earlier buildings including numerous little old houses and the former military parade ground near the Magazine Gateway. The municipal colleges of Art and Technology became the nucleus of this university in 1969 and it has since been expanded greatly. Its new buildings were designed by the City Architect's Department. The most conspicuous of them is the high-rise James Went Building with its slit windows irregularly spaced, over-looking the Newarke. It is named after Canon James Went who was headmaster of the Wyggeston Boys' school for 42 years.

YORK ROAD, the narrow street on the right, was named after the Duke of York, later James II (1633-1701). Round the corner, back in Oxford Street, is the **JAIN TEMPLE**, the only one of its kind in the western world. The Jains are a very old religious group - older than the Buddhists which they resemble. They revere Mahavira, who, like Buddha, achieved the state of perfection or nirvana. They do not worship Mahavira himself but all the good things he stands for. They believe in reincarnation and respect all forms of life and will not knowingly kill any living thing. The temple used to be a Congregational Church. The front has been completely covered in white marble richly carved in India. The interior was divided into two floors creating a community room on the ground floor with the temple above. Stained glass panels, illuminated from behind, illustrating scenes from the life of Mahavira, decorate the walls all round the main hall of the temple, the most holy part of which is filled with richly carved columns and arched ceilings. The superb glass and carving was all done in India to ensure that it was truly representational. Among the smaller rooms there is one devoted to the life of Mahatma Ghandi and another devoted to Mahavira, with a huge marble statue as the prominent feature.

The medieval **MAGAZINE GATEWAY** is on the left - we described it in some detail in our second armchair tour - and we now turn right into **NEWARKE STREET**, given this name by 1815 but called Hangman's Lane in 1741 because of the public executions which took place at the Magazine Gateway. On the right we pass the **ELFED THOMAS BUILDING**, now belonging to De Montfort University. It used to house the City's Education Offices but with the re-organisation of local government in 1974, the Leicestershire County Council's Education Committee became responsible for education in the whole of the county and this building was no longer needed for its original purpose. Elfed Thomas was the City's Director of Education.

Leicester's newest multi-deck red brick car park, which has been described as looking like a prison, dominates the area near Brown Street, with the **PHOENIX THEATRE** in the background. With the closing of the Palace, Leicester's last professional theatre, the only drama then presented came from the amateurs of the Little Theatre. The City Corporation agreed to meet the cost of building the Phoenix, a new small theatre which would be replaced by a larger permanent one later. The Haymarket Theatre was erected in 1973 but the Phoenix is still fulfilling a need.

As we come to the end of our final armchair tour in Welford Place, with the towering twin blocks of the New Walk Centre on the right and John Biggs's statue on the left, this is the time to reflect on the past of the ancient city. Counting the days when it was known as Ratae Corieltauvorum, Leicester has been in existence for two thousand years and this book has only just touched upon its history. Readers will find it most rewarding if they embark upon their own explorations and investigations.

105

OUT AND ABOUT IN LEICESTER

BIBLIOGRAPHY

–	Holy Trinity & its Surroundings, 1838-1966 (s.d.)
Billson C. J.	Mediaeval Leicester (1920)
Billson C.J. R.	Leicester Memoirs (1924)
Blank Elizabeth	Ratae Coritanorum (1971)
Bennett J. D.	Street Names of Leicester (1985)
Brandwood G. K.	Anglican Churches of Leicester (1983)
Chinnery G. A.	Leicester Castle & The Newarke (1981)
Docker Frances	John Paas & James Cook (s.d.)
Ellis Colin	History in Leicester (1969)
Elliott Malcolm	Victorian Leicester (1979)
Ekwall Eilert	Oxford Dictionary of Place Names (1936)
Fox Levi	"The Honor & Earldom of Leicester, 1066-1399" English Historical Revue Vol. LIV (1939)
	Leicester Castle (1944)
	Leicester Abbey (1971)
Fielding Johnson Mrs. T.	Glimpses of Ancient Leicester (1906)
Farquhar Jean	Arthur Wakerley, 1862-1931 (1984)
Farquhar J. & Skinner J.	The Turkey Cafe (1987)
Fosbrooke T. H. & Skillington S. H.	The Old Town Hall, Leicester (1925)
Gardiner William	Music & Friends (1838; 1853)
Greaves R. W.	The Corporation of Leicester, 1689-1836 (1970)
Green S. E. & Wilshere J.	Leicester Markets & Fairs (1973)
	The Siege of Leicester, 1645 (1970)
Gill Richard	The Book of Leicester (1985)
Halford Elizabeth	The Grand Old Man - Before & After (1984)
Hawton Gillian	The Story of Leicester Secular Society (1972)
Keene R. J. B.	Architecture in Leicester, 1834-1984 (1984)
Kelly William	The Great Mace & Other Corporation Insignia (1875)
	Drama & Amusements in Leicester (1865)
Leicestershire Museums	John Biggs (s.d.)
McKinley R. A. (ed.)	Victoria History of the County of Leicester, (Vol. IV) (1958)
Nichols John	The History and Antiquities of the County of Leicester, Vol. 1 Part 1 (1815)
Nash Andrew	A Brief Guide to St. Nicholas Church (s.d.)
Patterson A. Temple	Radical Leicester (1975)

107

Pegden N. A.	Leicester Guildhall (1981)
Reeve W. Napier	Chronicles of the Castle & of the Earls of Leicester (1867)
Simmons Jack	Leicester Past & Present Vols. 1 & 2 (1974)
	Life in Victorian Leicester (1971)
Skillington Florence	The Trinity Hospital (1982)
Skillington S. H.	A History of Leicester (1924)
Skillington F. E.	The Plain Man's History of Leicester (1950)
Throsby John	History of Leicester (1791)
Thompson J.	Handbook of Leicester (1859)
	The History of Leicester in the Eighteenth Century (1871)
	An Account of Leicester Castle (1859)
Tanner Michael	Crime & Murder in Victorian Leicester (1981)
Wheeler Keith	A Town Trail in Search of an Architect (s.d.)
Wilshere Jonathan	The Religious Gilds of Mediaeval Leicester (1979)
	Leicester Clock Tower (1974)
	The Town Gates & Bridges of Medieval Leicester (1978)
	The Town Halls of Leicester (1976)

OUT AND ABOUT IN LEICESTER

INDEX

Aethelfloeda 67, 95
Alderman Newton's School 24, 57
All Souls Church 102
Almond Road 101
Angel Gateway 54
Angel Inn 54, 64
Applegate Street 11
Assembly Rooms 57
Astley Clarke Building 99
Attenborough Building 98
Austin Friars 9
Aylestone Road 102

Balmoral House 87
Bear-baiting 20
Beaumont, Robert de 10
Bell Hotel 60
Belmont House Hotel 77
Belvoir Street 51
Benfield's House, Dr. 45
Berehill 56
Berridge Street 45
Biggs, John 82, 84
Biocentre 99
Bishop Street 47, 52
Black Anna 36
Blackfriars Pavement 13
Blue Boar Inn 28, 30
Blue Boar Lane 28
Bones 10, 16
Bonners Lane 103
Bow Bridge 9, 10
Bowling Green Street 47
Brigge, St Mary de (Our Lady of the Bridge) 10
Burley's Way 61
Butler, John Bridge 10
Butt Close Lane 63

Calais Hill 87
Calidaria (hot rooms) 14
Campbell Street 88

Castle, Leicester 36
Castle Gardens 33
Castle Park 33
Cardinal Telephone Exchange 59
Cathedral 21, 23
Cat Pye Gardens 51
Carts Lane 24
Cattle Market 45, 78, 101
Central Library 72
Central Police Station 89
Chancery Street 83
Chantry House 35, 36
Charles Street 58, 88, 89
Charles Wilson Building 98
Chatham Street 87
Cheapside 63
Church Gate 60, 63
Circuses 61
City Rooms 67
Clarence House 59
Clarence Street 60
Clinical Building 99
Clock Tower 56, 57, 60
Coal Hill 56, 57
College Street 91
Collegiate School 91, 92
Computer Centre 99
Conduit, The 64, 91
Conduit Street 64, 91
Constitutional Club 84
Cook, James 18, 72
Cook, Thomas 54, 73, 87, 90
Corn Exchange 65
Corn Wall 65
Corpus Christi - Feast of 17
Corpus Christi - Guild of 17, 18
Costume Museum 16
County Cricket 94
County Gaol 27
County Record Office 77
County Rooms 67
Cramant's Yard 80

Crescent, The	80
Crescent Cottages	80
Crown and Thistle	24
Danehills	36
Dead Lane	28
De Montfort Hall	96
De Montfort, Simon	57
De Montfort Street	77, 78, 92
De Montfort University	34, 103, 104
Dog Kennel Lane	51
Dover Street	87
Dr. Benfield's House	45
Earl's Market	64
East Gate	25, 60
East Gates Coffee House	60
East Midlands Gas	78
East Street	89
Elfed Thomas Building	104
Elizabeth House	88
Engineering Building	98
Every Street	47
Evington Road	94
Family Frypan	26
Fenton, John	22
Fenwick's Store	72
Fielding Johnson Building	98
Fielding Johnson Hospital	79
Fish Market	65
Fish and Quart	61
Football	94, 102
Fountain	46
Free Grammar School	28
Freeman, Hardy & Willis	59, 94
Freemen of the Borough of Leicester	73
Freemen's Common	99
Freeschool Lane	27
Friar Lane	44
Frigidarium	14
Gainsborough, The	65
Gallows/Gibbet	18, 94
Gallowtree Gate	53, 94
Gee Building, Percy	99
General News Room	51
Globe, The	24
Granby Halls	102
Granby Street	51, 87
Grand Hotel	51
Grange Lane	103
Granite Boulder	96
Granville Road	94
Guildhall	17
Guildhall Lane	17, 22, 24
Hall, Rev. Robert	77
Haymarket	57
Haymarket Centre	60
Haymarket Theatre	60, 104
High Cross	63, 80
High Street	25
Highcross Street	16, 26, 63
Highfield Street	93
Highfields	93
Holiday Inn	12, 13, 33
Holy Bones	15, 16
Holy Cross Church	75
Holy Trinity Church	80
Horsefair Street	45, 47, 71
Hotel Street	67
Humberstone Gate	58
Infirmary	102
Infirmary Close	102
Infirmary Road	102
Infirmary Square	103
Jain Temple	104
Jewry Wall	12, 13, 14
John of Gaunt's Cellar	38
Johnston, Dr. William	91
King Street	73, 80
Kyrkegate	60
Laconium (steam room)	14
Lambert, Daniel	11, 28, 43
Leicester Castle	36
Leicester Prison	79, 102
Leicester & Swannington Railway Company	9
Leicestershire Club	83
Leicestershire & Rutland Lunatic Asylum	97
Lewis's	58
London Road	88, 89, 93
Lord's Place	25

Loseby Lane 24
Lower New Walk 82

Magazine Gateway 43, 104
Mansfield Street 61
Market Centre 66
Market Place...64
Marlborough Street................................82
Marquis Street 80
May Fair..59
Medical Sciences Building 99
Memorial Arch 96
Mermaids 9
Michaelmas Fair.....................................59
Midland Bank...52
Mill Hill Lane...94
Million Pound Street.............................58
Mill Lane 103
Moot Hall..28
Morley Arcade 54
Murage Tax 12

National Westminster Bank..................52
Navigation Canal 11
Nelson Mandela Park..........................102
Nelson Street 92
New Street 23
New Walk...73
New Walk Centre 71, 82
New Walk Museum 76
Newarke 33, 42
Newarke Houses
   Museum.......................36, 41, 43, 103
Newarke Street 104
Newton, Gabriel 57
Newtown Street 79
Northampton Square 89
Nut Streets - Brazil..............................102
                    - Filbert...............................102
                    - Walnut 102

Oak trees..97
Oval, The 77
Oxford Street..103

Palace Theatre 60, 104
Palais de Danse 59
Park Hotel 93
Park International Hotel 59

Peace Walk 97
Peacock Lane 23
Pelham Street.......................................103
Pelican Inn 53
Peppermint Billy 79
Percy Gee Building 99
Pex Factory...10
Phoenix House 73
Phoenix Theatre...................................104
Pocklington's Walk 45, 83
Police Force..18
Police Station, Central..........................89
Pork Pie Chapel 71
Porridge Pot...35
Post Office 88
Prebend Street.......................................91
Prison, Leicester 79, 102

Queen Aethelfloeda 67, 95
"Queen Elizabeth's Pocket
Piece"..35

Race Course...94
Railway Station 91
Ratae Corieltauvorum 12, 104
Raw Dykes 14, 36, 102
Reference Library 47
Regent Road 78
Regent Street 92
Registry Office.......................................83
Richard III......................... 9, 23, 28, 33
River Soar...33
Robin Hood Public House 53
Roman Baths...14
Roman Catholic School 75
Royal Infirmary...................................102
Rupert's Gateway 36
Rutland Street 51

St. George Street 89
St. George's Church 89
St. George's Way....................................89
St. John the Divine Church.................77
St. Margaret's Church 61
St. Martin's Church..............................21
St. Martin's East 24
St. Martin's West 21
St. Mary de Castro Church 40
St. Mary's Field 102

St. Nicholas Church 15
St. Peter's Lane 61
St. Stephen's Presbyterian
Church 88
St. Stephen's United
Reformed Church 77
Sanvey Gate 61
Sawday Street 102
Saxby Street 92
Secular Hall 58
Shell-Mex Building 89
Shires, The 25
Silver Street 24
Singer Building 26
Skeffington House 43
Skeyth, The 61
Skulls 10
Smith, Francis "Tanky" 92
Soar, River 33
South African War Memorial 47
South Field 73, 74, 78, 89
Southfields College 101
South Gate 44
Southgates 44
Spa Place 59
Stephenson, Robert 9
Sunday School Centenary Hall 74
Swain Street 89
Swinesmarket 25

Tanky Smith 92
Temperance Hall 87, 96
Temperance Hotel 87
Temperance Society 54
Temple of Mithras 13
Tepid Baths 75
Tepidarium 14
Theatre Royal 68, 71
Three Cranes Inn 54
Three Crowns Inn 52
Tigers, The 43
Tolls 93
Top Hat Terrace 92
Town Hall 19, 20, 21, 45, 71
Town Hall Square 45, 46
Town Walls 53
Trams 60
Trinity Hospital 33, 45
Tudor Gatehouse 38

Turkey Cafe 52
Turret Gateway 35, 36

University of Leicester 97
University Road 77, 93
Upper King Street 80
Upper New Walk 77

Vaughan College 12, 15
Vestry Hall 58
Victoria Coffee House 51
Victoria Park 94, 97
Victoria Road Church 93

Wakerley, Arthur 91
War Memorial 96
Water Department Office 71
Waterloo Way 91
Weighbridge 59
Welford Place 73, 82, 104
Welford Road 99
Welford Road Cemetery 99
Wellington Street 72
Went, James 17
West Bridge 10, 11
West Gate 11
Whipping Toms 42
White Boar Inn 28
White Horse Inn 24
White, Sir Thomas 57
Wilson Building, Charles 98
Women's Lane 61
Wyggeston Collegiate Sixth Form
College 78, 92
Wyggeston Girls' School 59, 78, 92
Wyggeston Hospital 15, 23
Wyggeston Hospital Boys' School 17
Wyggeston, William 16, 23, 57, 66
Wygston, Roger 16, 20
Wygston's House 16, 17
Wyvern 65
Wyvern Hotel 89

York Road 104
York Street 87
Young Men's Christian Association 88